THE
PASSION
TRANSLATION

THE PASSIONATE LIFE BIBLE STUDY SERIES

T0246940

12-LESSON STUDY GUIDE

THE BOOK OF
JOSHUA

A New Beginning

tPt

BroadStreet
PUBLISHING

BroadStreet Publishing® Group, LLC
Savage, Minnesota, USA
BroadStreetPublishing.com

TPT: The Book of Joshua: 12-Lesson Bible Study Guide

9781424567553 (softcover)
9781424567560 (e-book)

Stock or custom editions of BroadStreet Publishing titles may be purchased in bulk for educational, business, ministry, fundraising, or sales promotional use. For information, please email info@broadstreetpublishing.com.

General editor: Brian Simmons
Managing editor: William D. Watkins
Writer: Matthew A. Boardwell

Design and typesetting by Garborg Design Works | garborgdesign.com

Printed in China

24 25 26 27 28 5 4 3 2 1

Contents

From God's Heart to Yours

"God is love," says the apostle John, and "Everyone who loves is fathered by God and experiences an intimate knowledge of him" (1 John 4:7). The life of a Christ-follower is, at its core, a life of love—God's love of us, our love of him, and our love of others and ourselves because of God's love for us.

And this divine love is reliable, trustworthy, unconditional, other-centered, majestic, forgiving, redemptive, patient, kind, and more precious than anything else we can ever receive or give. It characterizes each person of the Trinity—Father, Son, and Holy Spirit—and so is as limitless as they are. They love one another with this eternal love, and they reach beyond themselves to us, created in their image with this love.

How do we know such incredible truths? Through the primary source of all else we know about the one God—his Word, the Bible. Of course, God reveals who he is through other sources as well, such as the natural world, miracles, our inner life, our relationships (especially with him), those who minister on his behalf, and those who proclaim him to us and others. But the fullest and most comprehensive revelation we have of God and from him is what he has given us in the thirty-nine books of the Hebrew Scriptures (the Old Testament) and the twenty-seven books of the Christian Scriptures (the New Testament). Together, these sixty-six books present a compelling and telling portrait of God and his dealings with us.

It is these Scriptures that *The Passionate Life Bible Study Series* is all about. Through these study guides, we—the editors and writers of this series—seek to provide you with a unique and welcoming opportunity to delve more deeply into God's precious Word, encountering there his loving heart for you and all the others he loves. God wants you to know him more deeply, to love him more devoutly, and to share his heart with others more frequently and freely. To accomplish this, we have based this study guide series on The Passion Translation of the Bible, which strives to "reintroduce the passion and fire of the Bible to the English reader. It doesn't merely convey the literal meaning of words. It expresses God's passion for people and his world by translating the original, life-changing message of God's Word for modern readers." It has been created to "kindle in you a burning desire to know the heart of God, while impacting the church for years to come."[1]

In each study guide, you will find an introduction to the Bible book it covers. There you will gain information about that Bible book's authorship, date of composition, first recipients, setting, purpose, central message, and key themes. Each lesson following the introduction will take a portion of that Bible book and walk you through it so you will learn its content better while experiencing and applying God's heart for your own life and encountering ways you can share his heart with others. Along the way, you will come across a number of features we have created that provide opportunities for more life application and growth in biblical understanding.

 ## Experience God's Heart

This feature focuses questions on personal application. It will help you live out God's Word and to bring the Bible into your world in fresh, exciting, and relevant ways.

 ## Share God's Heart

This feature will help you grow in your ability to share with other people what you learn and apply in a given lesson. It provides guidance on using the lesson to grow closer to others and to enrich your fellowship with others. It also points the way to enabling you to better listen to the stories of others so you can bridge the biblical story with their stories.

The Backstory

This feature provides ancient historical and cultural background that illuminates Bible passages and teachings. It deals with then-pertinent religious groups, communities, leaders, disputes, business trades, travel routes, customs, nations, political factions, ancient measurements and currency…in short, anything historical or cultural that will help you better understand what Scripture says and means.

 Word Wealth

This feature provides definitions for and other illuminating information about key terms, names, and concepts, and how different ancient languages have influenced the biblical text. It also provides insight into the different literary forms in the Bible, such as prophecy, poetry, narrative history, parables, and letters, and how knowing the form of a text can help you better interpret and apply it. Finally, this feature highlights the most significant passages in a Bible book. You may be encouraged to memorize these verses or keep them before you in some way so you can actively hide God's Word in your heart.

 Digging Deeper

This feature explains the theological significance of a text or the controversial issues that arise and mentions resources you can use to help you arrive at your own conclusions. Another way to dig deeper into the Word is by looking into the life of a biblical character or another person from church history, showing how that man or woman incarnated a biblical truth or passage. For instance, Jonathan Edwards was well known for his missions work among native American Indians and for his intellectual prowess in articulating the Christian faith, Florence Nightingale for the reforms she brought about in healthcare, Irenaeus for his fight against heresy, Billy Graham for his work in evangelism, Moses for the strength God gave him to lead the Hebrews and receive and communicate the law, and Deborah for her work as a judge in Israel. This feature introduces to you figures from the past who model what it looks like to experience God's heart and share his heart with others.

The Extra Mile

While The Passion Translation's notes are extensive, sometimes students of Scripture like to explore more on their own. In this feature, we provide you with opportunities to glean more information from a Bible dictionary, a Bible encyclopedia, a reliable Bible online tool, another ancient text, and the like. Here you will learn how you can go the extra mile on a Bible lesson. And not just in study either. Reflection, prayer, discussion, and applying a passage in new ways provide even more opportunities to go the extra mile. Here you will find questions to answer and applications to make that will require more time and energy from you—if and when you have them to give.

As you can see above, each of these features has a corresponding icon so you can quickly and easily identify them.

You will find other helps and guidance through the lessons of these study guides, including thoughtful questions, application suggestions, and spaces for you to record your own reflections, answers, and action steps. Of course, you can also write in your own journal, notebook, computer document, or other resource, but we have provided you with space for your convenience.

Also, each lesson will direct you toward the introductory material and numerous notes provided in The Passion Translation. There each Bible book contains a number of aids supplied to help you better grasp God's words and his incredible love, power, knowledge, plans, and so much more. We want you to get the most out of your Bible study, especially using it to draw you closer to the One who loves you most.

Finally, at the end of each lesson you'll find a section called "Talking It Out." This contains questions and exercises for application that you can share, answer, and apply with your spouse, a friend, a coworker, a Bible study group, or any other individuals or groups who would like to walk with you through this material. As Christians, we gather together to serve, study, worship, sing, evangelize, and a host of other activities. We grow together, not just on our own. This section will give you ample opportunities to engage others with some of the content of each lesson so you can work it out in community.

We offer all of this to support you in becoming an even more faithful and loving disciple of Jesus Christ. A disciple in the ancient world was a student of her teacher, a follower of his master. Students study, and followers follow. Jesus' disciples are to sit at his feet and listen and learn and then do what he tells them and shows them to do. We have created *The Passionate Life Bible Study Series* to help you do what a disciple of Jesus is called to do.

So go.

Read God's words.

Hear what he has to say in them and through them.

Meditate on them.

Hide them in your heart.

Display their truths in your life.

Share their truths with others.

Let them ignite Jesus' passion and light in all you say and do.

Use them to help you fulfill what Jesus called his disciples to do: "Now wherever you go, make disciples of all nations, baptizing them in the name of the Father, the Son, and the Holy Spirit. And teach them to faithfully follow all that I have commanded you. And never forget that I am with you every day, even to the completion of this age" (Matthew 28:19–20).

And through all of this, let Jesus' love nourish your heart and allow that love to overflow into your relationships with others (John 15:9–13). For it was for love that Jesus came, served, died, rose from the dead, and ascended into heaven. This love he gives us. And this love he wants us to pass along to others.

Why I Love the Book of Joshua

Everyone needs a new beginning. When we fail, when a new year begins, or when we move into a new season of our lives, we want to start afresh. That's what the book of Joshua is all about. The death of Moses left everyone reeling. *What will happen now that Moses is gone? Who will lead us? Who will take us into the promised land?*, they wondered.

God wasted no time. After the time of grieving the loss of Moses, Yahweh spoke, essentially saying, "Joshua! You are the one who will take them in. Rise up! Be strong! And be fearless. I will be with you!" These are words every spiritual leader wants to hear from God: "I will be with you!"

Israel was at the threshold of moving into a promise they had received centuries before. Now it was time for Joshua to lead these under-forty adults into their inheritance.

I love the book of Joshua because it is filled with adventure and miracles as God wins life's battles. As long as God was with the Israelites and they obeyed the voice of the Lord, they would conquer. Joshua is a book that gives *me* the courage to move forward and the wisdom to keep leaning on God. There will be struggles of faith that will challenge the most stout-hearted among us, but God + nothing is enough.

I love Joshua because we find in its pages the ways of God, how he moves us forward, how we triumph over our enemies, and how we do the impossible. It is a book of action. The people go forward toward a flooding river, and it parts before their eyes. The people march around a city thirteen times, and the walls come tumbling down. The sun stands still, the enemies of God are conquered, cities bow before the power of Yahweh, and the hearts of God's people get filled with greater faith. If you feel like your days are filled with boredom, try reading the first few chapters of Joshua, and it will bring you into the battle of good versus evil.

I am thrilled as I read through the pages of Joshua because it truly fills me with courage. I need courage, and I feel like you who read this likewise need the infusion of courage to walk through the turbulent days we live in. Many modern believers act more like prisoners of war instead of passionate conquerors. We, as followers of Jesus, must see ourselves as "good soldiers" in God's army, prepared to fight spiritual battles (2 Timothy 2:3–5). The book of Joshua is a book of conquest, meant to embolden us to move from passivity to passion. Like Joshua, our battles are spiritual battles, for we fight not against flesh and blood but against forces of darkness.

So take heart, my friend! You will defeat your enemies and possess the promises God has given you. Nothing will defeat you as you follow the Commander of Angel Armies. I know you're going to love this study guide. Take the time to ponder each page and apply all that you learn.

God has courage he wants to impart to you, mighty one.

A new beginning is before you.

So seize the day!

Brian Simmons
General Editor

LESSON 1

The Prophet's Apprentice

(Various Scriptures)

From the east side of the Jordan River, Joshua prepared to embark on a military campaign. Almost a half millennia before, God promised Abram that the territory of Canaan would ultimately belong to his many descendants. Countless offspring? A permanent place to call home? To an old, childless desert nomad, this was almost too good to be true, but Abram believed God (Genesis 12:1–4; 15:1–21).

Abraham died in Canaan, and the only land he possessed was the plot he was buried in (25:7–10). Centuries would pass before his descendants would return to claim this promised land. In the intervening years, his promised children faced withering trials. Family strife, famine, emigration, chattel slavery, hostile armies, and wilderness wandering, each in their turn threatened the very survival of Abraham's lineage. But through God's faithfulness and intervention, Abraham's children returned to claim the promised land.

To settle this land, it would take a military conquest, and this included espionage, violence, and destruction. There were battle strategies and diplomatic treaties. There were glorious victories and humiliating defeats. And, as usual when people work in cooperation with God, there were miraculous interventions that accomplished divine purposes.

Therefore, we will embark on a spiritual campaign with these ancient people. In 1 Corinthians 10:1–13, Paul wrote that the experiences of Israel were recorded as encouragement, warnings, and examples for Christians. The history recorded in Joshua is a treasure trove of lessons for the followers of Jesus. We will witness the fledgling nation of Israel taking its first steps without Moses, experiencing firsthand the power and patience of God. We will learn from them as they choose to follow him into their rest.

A New Chapter Begins

"Marley was dead: to begin with. There is no doubt whatever about that. The register of his burial was signed by the clergyman, the clerk, the undertaker, and the chief mourner. Scrooge."[2] So begins Victorian England's most popular Christmas story.

From the first sentence of Dickens' classic, we learn that Jacob Marley's time had passed. He would influence the story, of course, but his chapter was over. Ebeneezer Scrooge was the next person named and the central character of the next chapter. His partnership with Marley and the reputation they forged together undergirded this well-worn tale.

Similarly, the opening lines of the biblical book of Joshua highlight two key leaders, Moses and Joshua. "After Moses, Yahweh's servant, died, Yahweh spoke to Joshua son of Nun, Moses' faithful assistant" (Joshua 1:1). Moses' chapter was closed, and with his passing, Joshua became the central figure of the next chapter in the story of God's covenant people Israel. Scripture had never mentioned Joshua by name without reference to Moses. For decades they were inseparable. Death had now separated these two men, and Joshua had to go forward alone at the head of this nomad nation as they secured their new homeland.

Joshua's leadership skills did not materialize suddenly. His experiences as a common Israelite and then companion to Moses forged Joshua's character and competence. He established his place in the hearts of his fellow Israelites as Israel's undisputed leader of the conquest through many years of challenges together and through his steadfast faith.

An Israelite

Abraham, Isaac, and Jacob were the first fathers of this people. In their lifetimes, there was no nation of Israel for them to belong to. Moses was an Israelite but exceptional in his infancy, upbringing, and calling. When he arose as a deliverer, he was decidedly an outsider. However, before Joshua made a name for himself among the covenant people of God, he was a common member of that nation. So before considering the events that distinguish Joshua from his people, let's review the soul-forming experiences he shared with them.

Like all Jacob's descendants of his generation, Joshua was born a slave. He was born under the oppressive rule of the Egyptian pharaoh who had no regard for God or his covenant people. Exodus 1:6–22 describes the cruelty and hopelessness of this era for Israel.

- *This new pharaoh mentions specific concerns he has about this immigrant community in Egypt. What did he worry about (Exodus 1:8–10)?*

- *What three strategies did Pharaoh employ to diminish the Israelite population in Egypt?*

- *Who had to cooperate with him to accomplish these strategies (vv. 11, 15, 22)? Did they cooperate?*

Joshua was born about a generation after this oppression began. He was a forced laborer, toiling to turn raw materials into buildings, temples, pyramids, and monuments. His Egyptian masters channeled his efforts to build the Egyptian empire, honor Egyptian culture, and worship Egyptian gods. This was an inauspicious beginning for a man who would rise to lead the people of the one true God.

Like the rest of Israel, Joshua was delivered from slavery through the miraculous intervention of God. When Moses recounted the wonders of God that led Israel to the edge of the promised land, he reminded them of the slavery they came from and especially how God set them free (Deuteronomy 7:7–19). Moses expected all the generations that followed to remember these wonders.

- *How did Moses describe Israel's unpromising beginnings (Deuteronomy 7:7)?*

• *What motivated God to come to their rescue (v. 8)?*

• *What miraculous troubles did God inflict on Israel's oppressors (vv. 15, 19)? How does God describe his power in setting the Hebrews free (vv. 8, 19)?*

• *Was it Israel's strength that broke them out of bondage? Was it Israel's strength that would enable them to conquer the promised land?*

- *What did Moses expect his people to conclude from the wonders God showed them in Egypt (vv. 18–19)?*

Joshua, like all his countrymen, walked through the Red Sea on dry ground (Exodus 14:13–31). Getting free from Egypt was the first step; staying free was the next. When Pharaoh changed his mind and chased down the newly freed slaves with his army, the Hebrews were trapped against the sea. Everyone expected a slaughter and re-enslavement, but God showed his power again.

- *Did Israel have to fight Egypt for their freedom? Did they have to defend themselves (Exodus 14:13–14)?*

- *What sequence of miracles did God perform to rescue them in this instance (vv. 19–20, 21, 24–25, 27–28)?*

- *How did the Egyptian army bring glory to God (vv. 17–18)?*

- *What effect did this miracle have in the hearts of the Hebrews (vv. 30–31)?*

With the rest of his people, Joshua spent forty years of his life wandering in the wilderness (Deuteronomy 8:1–9). When they could have been conquering and settling, they were condemned to wandering tantalizingly close to the promised land, facing the elements, and living in tents.

- *What did God plan to accomplish through the wilderness wanderings of the Hebrews (Deuteronomy 8:2, 5)?*

- *How did God provide for their physical needs in the wilderness (vv. 3–4)?*

- *The contrast was stark between resources in the wilderness and the promised land. What did their new homeland have that they lacked in the wilderness (vv. 7–9)?*

- *What did God demand of the Hebrews, whether they were wandering or settled in the new land (vv. 1, 6)?*

Joshua shared in all these experiences as an ordinary citizen of Israel. He was part of the national identity shaped by slavery, deliverance, walking through the sea, and God's provision in the wilderness. The lessons he learned from these common experiences informed the rest of his life as a leader of God's people.

🔲 WORD WEALTH

Joshua actually has two names in the Bible. In Numbers 13:8, he is called Hoshea, the son of Nun. A handful of verses later, we read that Moses changed his name to Joshua (v. 16). This name is more than a tag identifying the man. It is the description of his life's work and a reminder about the nature of his God.

His birth name Hoshea, pronounced /hoe-SHAY-uh/, means "salvation." When Nun placed this name on his infant son, born into bondage, he expressed hope for a rescue. Maybe this generation would be free. Moses' change to his name was slight but important. Joshua means "the LORD is salvation." Altering his name moved the meaning from a vague hope to the certain source of that hope. The salvation the Hebrews longed for was realized in the Lord Yahweh. He alone could deliver them. He alone saved them. Joshua would wear this declaration for the rest of his life.

Centuries later, when an angel visited Joseph, the fiancé of Mary, with miraculous challenging news, this name is used purposefully once again. "She will give birth to a son, and you are to give him the name Jesus, because he will save his people from their sins" (Matthew 1:21 NIV). The NIV footnote reads, "*Jesus* is the Greek form of *Joshua*, which means *the* LORD *saves*." Like Joshua, Jesus would have heard this confident declaration every time his mother called him for dinner, whenever a villager addressed him, or when individuals cried out to him for help and healing. He was the living embodiment of the Lord saving. He came to be our Savior from sin.

An Old Testament historical book called "Jesus" should perk up our spiritual ears. As we make our way through this book with this remarkable title, we will see some remarkable parallels for God's covenant people. By God's personal intervention, we receive his promises of salvation and spiritual rest.

A Military Captain

The first time that the Bible mentions Joshua by name is when the Amalekites muster an army to confront Israel on their journey from Egypt to Sinai (Exodus 17:8–16). These emigrants walking through their territory must have seemed an easy target, so the Amalekites came out to stop them. Like jackals, they preyed on the stragglers when they were "weary and worn out" (Deuteronomy 25:17–18 NIV). Moses turned to Joshua to lead the Hebrews in their first military battle.

- *What sign showed the Hebrews that their victory did not depend on military might alone (Exodus 17:9–12)?*

- *In previous victories, Yahweh won without participation from the Hebrews. The plagues, the angel of death, and the Red Sea crossing were all God at work without human cooperation. Why do you think his plan included Joshua and an army this time (vv. 13–15)?*

- *What lessons could Joshua take from this experience to later lead Israel, the young nation of Hebrews?*

A True Worshiper

In one of the most despicable episodes in Israel's history, Joshua alone stood apart with Moses (Exodus 32:1–35). As Moses was up on Mount Sinai communicating with the Lord for them, the other Hebrews were swept up in an idolatrous frenzy. As Moses sought the one true God, they manufactured a false one. While Yahweh commanded in writing that there be no other gods and no graven images, they worshiped both with uncontrolled debauchery.

Where was Joshua during this national moral disaster? He was faithfully attending to Moses on the mountain.

- *Why did the Israelites decide to make the golden calf (Exodus 32:1, 4)?*

- *Who helped the nation commit this appalling sin (vv. 2–5)? Did this person take any responsibility for his part in it (vv. 21–24)?*

- *How did they worship this new god of theirs (vv. 6, 18, 25)? How do these activities compare to the worship of the true God?*

- *Where was Joshua when all this was happening (24:13; 32:15–18)?*

- *Is it important that Joshua and Moses were not part of this wicked party? Why might it matter?*

When the people moved off from their encampment at Mount Sinai, Moses set up a tent where he could meet personally with God (33:7–11). This tent of meeting became a kind of office for Moses, where people could come to him for guidance from God. Not surprisingly, we find Joshua there too.

- *What was the purpose of this tent (33:7)? What did Moses do while he was in the tent (v. 11)?*

- *What symbols showed the people that Yahweh's special presence was with Moses in this place (vv. 9–10)?*

• *Where could Moses' young apprentice Joshua always be found (v. 11)?*

• *What do these experiences of seeking God alongside Moses imply about Joshua?*

A Faithful Scout

From the foot of Mount Sinai, the people of Israel slowly made their way up the Arabian Peninsula through the regions east of the Jordan River and camped on Jordan's banks looking across into Canaan. Then Moses sent a team of twelve scouts ahead to investigate what the land was like and what challenges they might face (Numbers 13–14). Joshua was one of these men.

• *Who planned this exploration (Numbers 13:1–2)?*

- *What questions did Moses want the scouts to answer about the land (vv. 17–20)?*

- *What amazing trophy did they return with as evidence of the plentiful land (vv. 23–24, 26–27)?*

- *How long did they explore the entire land of Canaan (v. 25)?*

- *What did most of the spies think about the prospects of conquering the inhabitants (vv. 28–29, 31–33)? What did Joshua and Caleb think about it (v. 30; 14:6–9)?*

- *Whose report did the people trust (14:1–4, 10)? What did they decide to do?*

- *What were the consequences of their decision not to enter the land (vv. 28–35)? How long would the people wander (vv. 33–34)? Why so long?*

For forty days, Joshua and his companions explored the promised land and determined that it was indeed a rich land where they could prosper. However, only he and Caleb had enough confidence in God to charge ahead with the conquest. They walked the same distance, saw the same sights, encountered the same inhabitants, but came to radically different conclusions. By faith, Joshua and Caleb were ready to obey God's command to conquer. As a result, they would be the only men of their generation to enter Yahweh's promised land.

An Appointed Successor

Even heroes die. As important as Moses the lawgiver was, his era of history had to end. Thankfully, he had a loyal apprentice alongside him who had been with him a long time. For many years, Joshua watched and learned while Moses led this stubborn nation. He had been a faithful aide to Moses through many trials. When it came time to pass the baton, Joshua was close at hand and well prepared.

• *What was Moses' final ministry to Joshua as he prepared to transfer leadership to him (Deuteronomy 3:27–28)?*

• *When Moses brought Joshua in front of the people to appoint him, what commands did he give him (31:7–8)? What assurances did he give (v. 8)?*

• *What final ministry did Moses and Joshua do together for the people (32:44–46)?*

These experiences prepared Joshua to lead a new era, *his* era, of Israel's history. As an ordinary Hebrew, he learned God's power to free, to rescue, and to provide. As an aide to Moses, he learned God's power to conquer, to counsel, and to reveal. He was Spirit-filled and ready.

> If we…want to be used in the Lord's
> work, we must be ready for a time of
> preparation. Usually there is preparation
> before leadership. Both Moses and Joshua
> had many, many years of preparation…God
> taught Joshua all these things as Joshua
> followed Moses in the wilderness. Then, with
> these lessons learned, Joshua was ready to
> lead the people into the promised land.[3]

 EXPERIENCE GOD'S HEART

- *Joshua was no Moses, but he didn't need to be. God wanted Joshua, not Moses, to lead the next chapter of Israel's history. List some key differences between Joshua and Moses. Why were these unique qualities a benefit to Joshua as he led Israel into the promised land?*

- *Sometimes the chapter endings of life are obvious: the death of a loved one, a professional promotion or dismissal, a championship victory, a life-changing health incident, an educational credential, and the like. Think about some chapter endings in your life. What did God teach you in the previous chapter of your life to prepare you for the new era that followed?*

❤ SHARE GOD'S HEART

- *As you consider those chapter closing moments, there may be a person in your life who would be encouraged by your experience. Ask God to bring to your mind a person who might like to hear your story. Pray that the opportunity will open for that very soon.*

- *It is likely that someone you know is in the middle of a difficult chapter transition right now. For them, this is a season of loss or hardship. Pray for them. Pray that they will have the strength and courage to face what is happening and what is to come. Pray that God will surface the principles they need for the next chapter.*

Talking It Out

Since Christians grow in community, not just in solitude, every "Talking It Out" section contains questions you may want to discuss with another person or in a group. Here are the exercises for this lesson.

1. Large groups are often swayed by fear rather than hope. Even with an enthusiastic and confident leader like Joshua or Caleb in the mix, people can be reluctant to move ahead with confidence. Talk about some examples. Discuss why you think this occurs.

2. Joshua received great benefit from observing Moses' friendship with God. This example must have wielded lifelong influence over Joshua. Tell the others in the group about an individual who has profoundly influenced your spiritual life. What major lesson did they teach you about the Lord or about yourself?

LESSON 2

Inauguration Day

(Deuteronomy 31–Joshua 1)

The peaceful transition of leadership is arguably one of the most ingenious aspects of American government. Every two years, voters are offered the potential to affirm or correct the direction of the country, with the entire House of Congress and one-third of the Senate membership up for grabs. But popularly seen as the most important national election is that of the US president, a chief executive for all the people. The campaign for the election of this leader captures national attention in a way no other political contest can.

When the electoral votes are counted and the vote certified, plans get underway for the elected president's inauguration.[4] What guests will be present? Where will they sit? Who will participate in the ceremony? How much of the general public will be admitted, and what will the security arrangements be? While the details are different from one personality to another, some components are consistent.

The inauguration ceremony has always sought to demonstrate support for the new leader from the previous administration, the public, and God. In the case of a president's first term, a representative of the prior administration will attend to personally illustrate the transition. Members of both political parties, even some former or future presidential rivals, showcase their desire for unity going forward. Finally, even in an increasingly secular republic, a Bible, a prayer, and a promise invoking God affirm the president's dependence on Divine Providence. These components of every inauguration help to legitimize the new leader.

As the book of Joshua opens, these support-lending components were necessary for Joshua's ascension to leadership too. As Moses' successor, he needed Moses' endorsement. As the leader of God's covenant people, he needed the approval of God. And as the head of a nation with an enormous task ahead, he needed the cooperation of other leaders. At this key turning point, he needed to be confirmed.

Moses' Endorsement

When marketers want the public to have confidence in a new product, they will often recruit a well-known personality to endorse it. These celebrity endorsements help consumers trust the product until it proves its worth through direct experience. A familiar, trusted face makes up for the lack of a track record.

While Joshua had a track record in Israel, he also had a larger-than-life predecessor. How would people's loyalties shift from the prophet to the prophet's sidekick?

From the beginning, Joshua's credibility as a leader stemmed from his relationship with Moses. For a generation, he had been Moses' aide and companion. An endorsement from Moses would be a tremendous help. Thankfully, he got it. Joshua could take up his new role in the nation with confidence because Moses had confidence in him.

- *Who witnessed Moses' handoff of authority to Joshua (Deuteronomy 31:7)?*

- *What character qualities did Moses command Joshua to exhibit (vv. 7–8)? Why would Joshua need these qualities?*

- *What assurances did Moses give to Joshua about the Lord's involvement in the mission ahead of him (v. 8)?*

- *What ritual did Moses perform so that Israel saw his public approval of Joshua as leader (34:9)? What spiritual result came from that ritual? How did the people respond to Moses' endorsement?*

 # THE BACKSTORY

To judge from Hollywood productions, you might think that Moses was the undisputed leader of Israel out of Egypt and through the wilderness to the promised land. The reality is that, even though God himself called, sent, and empowered Moses to deliver them, Moses faced fierce opposition during his leadership. The examples are so many that when Moses recounts his history with them, he sums it up like this: "I know how rebellious and stiff-necked you are. If you have been rebellious against the Lord while I am still alive and with you, how much more will you rebel after I die!" (31:27 NIV).

- *Read the following examples of people opposing Moses. What were the reasons they were dissatisfied with him? How did their opposition resolve? What lessons can we learn from the conflict?*

Passage	Moses' Opposition	Complaint	Resolution	Lessons Learned
Exodus 5:15–23				
Exodus 6:6–9				
Exodus 14:10–14				

Exodus 15:22–27				
Exodus 16:2–18				
Exodus 17:1–7				
Numbers 12				
Numbers 14:36–45				
Numbers 16				
Numbers 21:4–9				

- *Incidentally, the Israelites never grumbled or rebelled against Joshua during his long leadership over them. Do you suppose the affirmations he received from the outset of his leadership had anything to do with that? Why or why not?*

God's Approval

As important as Moses' endorsement was to Joshua's leadership, the approval of Yahweh was immeasurably more so. Joshua was about to embark on a mission that had always been the priority of God more than anyone else.

It was God who called Abraham out of his own comfortable family setting and brought him to this land in the first place. It was God who prospered him there. It was God who promised the land to Abraham hundreds of years before. It was God who sent Moses and then plagues to deliver Abraham's descendants from Egyptian slavery. It was God who gave them the law to govern a new way of life at Mount Sinai. It was God who led and cared for them through the wilderness to the edge of the Jordan.

Joshua was on the cusp of fulfilling God's plan. He needed God's approval more than that of anyone else. Again, thankfully, he was God's appointed leader for this task.

- *Whom did God choose specifically to lead Israel into the promised land (Deuteronomy 31:14)?*

- *What visible signal showed witnesses that the Lord was present at Joshua's commissioning (vv. 14–15)?*

- *How did God describe the task that Joshua was to perform (v. 23)? What character qualities did the Lord demand of him to do it? What personal promise did God give him for the task?*

This initial handoff took place while Moses still lived. It was one of the prophet's final official acts as leader of Israel. However, the book of Joshua opens after Moses' death and the Israelites had completed their days of mourning. With such a devastating recent loss and such a daunting task ahead, anyone might be reluctant to get started again. So God himself pushed the conquest forward.

- *What blunt announcement did Yahweh make to initiate the start of this new chapter in Israel's history (Joshua 1:2)? What did Joshua and the people need to prepare to do?*

- *The Lord gave two descriptions of the land they could lay claim to. One described the degree to which Israel would cooperate with God's plan. How could they cooperate (1:3)?*

- *The other description included physical land features. What are they (v. 4)? Is there any discrepancy between these two descriptions? What might explain the difference?*

- *What did God say about Joshua's enemies in the conquest (v. 5)?*

- *What promises did the Lord make to show he would continue the work of Moses (vv. 5, 9)?*

- *God repeated a charge to Joshua that he made previously in the commissioning with Moses. What was it (vv. 6, 7, 9)?*

- *Next, God pointed Joshua to a brand-new resource that would help him carry out his task. What was this resource (vv. 7–8)?*

- *What condition did God place on Joshua's prosperity and success in the conquest? Which phrases show how devoted Joshua was to be to the law of Moses (vv. 7–8)?*

Public Confirmation

Joshua's commissioning was public, so the people were aware of the mantle of leadership that Moses and God laid on him. Again, this was God's plan, and Joshua was God's man. With Moses' endorsement and God's approval, all that remained was for the people to follow him.

So Joshua gave his first order, and the people began to stir from their grief to get ready to cross the river. It would not be long before their feet would be treading the ground that God wanted them to claim for their own. But there was one group of Israelites, the Reubenites and Gadites, who were already standing on their own land.

 # THE BACKSTORY

During the forty years of wilderness wanderings, the Israelites came into conflict with some of the inhabitants east of the Jordan. Millions of emigrants traveling through their territory were perceived as threats to the locals. The Aradites (Numbers 21:1–3), King Sihon of the Amorites (vv. 21–32), and King Og of Bashan (vv. 33–35) mustered their armies and attacked Israel as they passed through on their journey. Fledgling Israel successfully defended themselves. Ultimately, they defeated all three kings and their people and took over their territories.

The leaders of the Reubenites and Gadites, two of the largest tribes of Israel, noted that these newly emptied pastures were adequate for the needs of their livestock and that the conquered cities could easily house the people of their tribes. So they asked Moses if they could possess these lands as their inheritance rather than waiting for territory inside Canaan (32:1–5).

At first, this made Moses angry. He believed that by peeling off in their own direction to settle these lands, the tribes were abandoning the rest of Israel to fight the conquest without them (vv. 6–7). He thought they were drawing back from crossing the Jordan into Canaan out of the same fear and disobedience that kept their fathers from taking the land (vv. 8–15).

The Reubenites and Gadites understood Moses' objections but assured him of their military support and confidence in God. They still wanted to leave their flocks and families behind in the land east of the Jordan, but they offered to go ahead of the rest of the army into the promised land to fight Israel's enemies. They would not return home until God had granted the rest of the nation victory and the other tribes were settling into their own lands (vv. 16–19).

Moses agreed to this plan and granted the already conquered lands east of the Jordan to the Reubenites, the Gadites, and the Manassehites. Then he made these tribes swear an oath that they would follow through on this plan. If they kept their promise, this ground would become their inheritance. If they did not, then their lands would be forfeit (vv. 20–32).

In the years since that agreement, these Transjordan tribes had begun to settle. They drove out the inhabitants, claimed their possessions, and built up their cities. Their families lived in houses, and their flocks grazed the fields. These tribes were happily settled in when Joshua issued the order to prepare to cross over into the promised land. If anyone would have been unhappy to move on, if anyone might have been resistant to this order, it would have been the Reubenites, the Gadites, and the Manassehites. This was Joshua's moment of truth, his first test of leadership.

- What arrangement did Joshua remind the Transjordan tribes about (Joshua 1:12–15)?

- What portion of their tribes had to be involved with the invasion (vv. 13–14)?

- How long would they have to fight for their fellow Israelites before returning home (v. 15)?

- Did the Reubenite, Gadite, and Manassehites agree again to these terms? What commands of Joshua were they willing to obey (v. 16)?

- *Where were they willing to go? How much loyalty were they offering to Joshua (vv. 16–18)?*

- *What familiar charge did they give Joshua (v. 18)?*

Strength and Courage

Repeatedly in these commissioning passages, Joshua was given this charge: Be strong and courageous!

- *Why do you think that Moses, God, and the Israelites all urged Joshua on with these words (Deuteronomy 31:6–7, 23; Joshua 1:6–7, 9, 18)?*

- *Why is it significant that it always comes as a command?*
  Does Joshua have a choice to make? Support your answer.

The prevalence of this instruction is not to say that Joshua was a weak or fearful man. By this time, he had already demonstrated his willingness to go to battle. For years, he had shown stalwart support for Moses. And when it came time to enter the land the first time, he was one of just two men in the whole country who were courageous enough to charge forward with the help of God.

These qualities would be invaluable for the task ahead. No weak or weak-willed leader would be able to do it. No timid or fearful leader would even try.

The conquest would offer many opportunities for fear. A river at flood stage to cross. Cities with walls so fortified that breaching them seemed impossible. Established and respected kings joining forces to attack Israel. In those moments, weakness and fear would be the natural human response. However, knowing God's plan and trusting his promises, Joshua could choose strength and courage in the face of all the dangers to come.

Priority for Scripture

For the modern Christian with multiple Bibles scattered around the house, it may be impossible to understand what a treasure Joshua held in his hands. The book of the Law (the Torah) was a resource the world had never known before. The black-and-white, written words of God collected in one place to be read and consulted was a brand-new thing.

Histories had been written before. In fact, the first portion of what Moses had collected was probably histories others had recorded. The accounts of Adam, Noah, Shem, Terah, Esau, Abraham, and Jacob make up most of what we call Genesis.[5] Religious ideas had been recorded before. These histories mention many moments of divine revelation and key turning points for the people of God.

What was new about the Torah was its thorough description of the righteous standards of God. This was a guide for almost every area of life: political leadership, religious rituals, moral duty, societal ideals, hygiene practices, dietary limits, rules of warfare, responsibility to the poor, and so on. The Torah spelled out all these things in specific terms for a nation only beginning to form its own culture.

If Joshua wanted to carry on the leadership ministry of Moses, if he wanted the permanent approval of God, he would need to lead these people to embrace this way of life. He would have to read the words, know and understand the words, practice and love the words in this Law. Success for him as a leader depended on his deepening relationship with God's written revelation.

Believers still depend on the written word of God. The gospel explains God's solution for our estrangement from him because of sin (Matthew 1:21), but how do we know what sin is? Scripture tells us (Romans 7:7). Ultimately, salvation is about new life in Christ, but where do we learn about this good news? In Scripture (1 Corinthians 15:2–4). As we grow in Christ, the Holy Spirit reminds us of his teachings (John 14:26), but where are those teachings recorded? Scripture. When we want to know for certain that we hear from God, we read his words in Scripture.

Promise of Success

With the supportive affirmation of Moses, the people, and Yahweh himself, Joshua began his life's great work. He did not have to wonder if God would be with him. That was explicitly promised to him. He did not have to wonder if God would counsel him throughout the campaign. He was holding the written words of God. He did not have to wonder if he could finish the task. Prosperity, success, and victory were assured.

Joshua only needed to be strong and very courageous.

 EXPERIENCE GOD'S HEART

- *What confidence Joshua must have had knowing that his mentor Moses approved of him! Have you ever needed the endorsement of a predecessor for a new position? Did you receive it? What happened when you did or did not?*

- *Written Scripture is the objective source of all the spiritual truth we know. Many Christians rely on daily Bible reflection to sustain their spiritual lives. What Bible reading, meditating, or memorizing habits do you have? How often do you meet with others to discuss what you read in God's Word?*

- *We take new ground when we tell new people the gospel. We take new ground when we break old habits of bondage. We take new ground when we step forward in faith to accomplish a new God-prompted task. What difference does it make to know that Yahweh "will never fail nor abandon you" (Joshua 1:5) or that he will be "with you every day, even to the completion of this age" (Matthew 28:20)?*

 SHARE GOD'S HEART

- *Life is full of disappointments and challenges. Many people endure these hardships silently, without ever letting another soul know what they are going through. In those difficult moments, words of affirmation can often buoy someone's spirit. Who do you know that could use a truthful word of encouragement from you? Make a plan to share that word with them.*

Talking It Out

1. Select someone from the group to encourage. Ask them what challenges they are facing right now and what personal qualities or resources God has given them to meet the challenge. Remind them of God's personal presence in that situation. Read to them specific Scripture verses that are helpful to you or that have come to mind during their sharing. Then pray for them together.

2. What does it take to be a leader today? What are the character qualities of a leader whom people can have confidence in following? Discuss these questions, including in light of what you have learned so far about Joshua and his preparation for leadership.

LESSON 3

A Scarlet Cord

(Joshua 2)

The *ribba-dibba-dibba-dak!* of a hairy woodpecker cracks through the quiet of the morning forest, its jackhammer head blasting through the bark of an ponderosa pine. An iridescent hummingbird rockets past, leaving musical tones in the wake of its supersonic wings. Nearby, a half-dozen bluey-grey, dark-eyed juncos scrounge for seeds beneath the wooden birdfeeder. What an astounding array of colors and sounds, abilities and design in such a small plot of ground!

And that's just a taste of the range of bird species from a single locale. Consider that a rhea, a lovebird, a roadrunner, a flamingo, and a penguin are all part of this diverse class of winged creatures.

There are as many distinctions as there are species among birds, but they all have one unifying trait: feathers. Whether the water and ice shedding feathers of a penguin or the mating display feathers of the peacock or the soaring feathers of the albatross, no bird is without them.

Conversion stories come in a wide variety of species too. Ask a roomful of believers to share how they came into the Christian faith, and you are likely to hear some truly unique stories. Maybe one was a child who heard the good news of Jesus in Sunday school and believed. Maybe another was a stubborn rebel, who, after years of resistance, repented. Maybe another was an avowed atheist, but gradually their heart was changed. Whatever the differences, there will be one commonality: faith.

You would be hard-pressed to find a more unique and unlikely conversion story than that of Rahab of Jericho. Her story is recorded once but remembered twice in the New Testament as an inspiration for the children of God. After thousands of years, she remains an extraordinary witness to God's heart for rescuing sinners from all nations.

Checking It Out

Read Joshua 2 and then answer the following questions.

- *Who sent the spies into the land? How many went (Joshua 2:1)? How many faithful spies scouted out the land the first time Israel came to the promised land (Numbers 14:6–8)? Do you think there is any significance in that similarity? If so, what is it?*

- *What city was Joshua especially interested in learning about? Where did the spies find shelter? What does the Bible say about their host?*

- *When the king learned that there were spies in his city, where did he send his messengers to look? Why do you suppose he thought he would find the strangers there (Joshua 2:2–3)?*

- *List three things Rahab did to help the spies she sheltered (vv. 4–8). Did her ploy work?*

Rahab was a prostitute. There is nothing in the Joshua account to indicate that she entertained these men sexually,[6] but the Bible almost always identifies her by her trade (Joshua 2:1; 6:25; Hebrews 11:31; James 2:25). We should probably think of her lodgings like a hostel where travelers might find shelter (and other services, if desired) rather than a brothel.

The Canaanites were notorious for their sexual immorality. This was one of the major indictments God made against them when he promised Abraham their land. Even in Abraham's time, the sexual behavior of these people was nauseating (Genesis 13:13; 19:1–11; 34:1–4; 38:13–26), and in the law of Moses, their sexual practices were explicitly listed as one reason for the forfeiture of their land (Leviticus 18). Still, God was patient with them, giving them hundreds of years to repent and course-correct (Genesis 15:12–16).

As God's holy people, we would not expect Israel's first personal interaction in the promised land to be with a prostitute, but such is the extravagant grace of God. Of course, God would save Israel, but he was also willing to save sinners from all the nations.

- *What did the spies tell Rahab about God? How did she already know so much about him (Joshua 2:10)?*

- *What are the two things Rahab said she knew about the Lord (vv. 9, 11)?*

- *What two miracles that God performed were the basis of the Canaanites' feelings toward Israel (v. 10)?*

- *How did Rahab describe the state of mind of the people in Jericho (vv. 9, 11)?*

- *What could the spies conclude from her confession?*

Intriguingly, the spies did not tell Rahab about the Lord. They did not come to tell her about God's power to save. They did not come to tell her about their miraculous deliverance from Egypt or the crossing of the Red Sea. They did not come to tell her how Joshua led them in victory against the kings across the Jordan. They came to discover the keys to defeating her people. But they did not have to tell her. She already knew all these things!

Who told her about their God if they didn't? The grapevine. When each of these miraculous events happened, word got around. For forty years, Canaanites had been talking about it. Certainly, that was long enough for every local to hear about this throng of nomadic strangers whose God had humbled local kings and the mighty Egyptian pharaoh. If others were no match for this God, what would become of the Canaanites? This frightened pagan prostitute heard about Yahweh, the God of Israel, from other frightened pagans.

# THE EXTRA MILE

God is so creative in getting his message out. Usually, he uses willing and obedient followers to spread his good news, but the Bible is full of unusual methods too. Read the following passages and take note of the methods and the messengers that God used to communicate with people.

Passage	Method	Message	Receiver
Exodus 3:1–10			
2 Kings 5:1–14			
2 Chronicles 34:10–20			
Daniel 5			
Matthew 2:1–12			
Luke 2:8–20			

Acts 8:26–39			
Acts 9:1–9			
Acts 10:9–23			

Faith Changes Our Loyalties

Confronted with this awe-inspiring gossip, Rahab had to decide: Did she believe it? Believing would irreversibly change her life. If the Lord was who he seemed to be, the God over heaven and earth, then she was no less his subject than the Israelite spies. If he was the God of all peoples, she needed to side with him even if it meant treason against her own people. It would be foolhardy to oppose God. So when her king sent for the spies, when his men pursued them, she protected them.

Many believers today still place loyalty to God before their own people and family. In a believing family, it isn't always necessary. Sometimes the whole community is delighted when one of their children trusts in Jesus Christ. Sadly, this is not always the case.

For example, when Zahid, a Muslim militant from Pakistan, persecuted a Christian, confiscated his Bible, and secretly read it, he surprisingly converted to faith in Christ. After this, his loyalties flipped completely.

> All he wanted to do was share Jesus with everyone he knew. He went to his family

members and those in the mosque and told them what had happened to him… but they didn't believe him. His family and friends turned against him. They called the authorities to have him arrested so he would leave them alone about his Jesus. According to Islamic teaching, Zahid was now considered an apostate, a traitor to Islam, a man who had turned from his faith and accepted stupid lies. Thus, he was a criminal…"Although I suffered greatly at the hands of my Muslim captors, I held no bitterness toward them. I knew that just a few years before, I had been one of them."[7]

It may seem bizarre to risk one's life and relationships for God's sake, but we should expect it. When we must make a choice between God and any other attachment, we must follow him. Jesus said it would happen.

Perhaps you think I've come to spread peace and calm over the earth—but my coming will bring conflict and division, not peace. Because of me, a son will turn against his father, a daughter her mother and against her mother-in-law. Within your own families you will find enemies. Whoever loves father or mother or son or daughter more than me is not fit to be my disciple. And whoever comes to me must follow in my steps and be willing to share my cross and experience it as his own, or he is not worthy of me. Those who cling to their lives will give up true life. But those who let go of their lives for my sake and surrender it all to me will discover true life! (Matthew 10:34–39)

Rahab was in this situation. The Lord of all the peoples had revealed himself to her through the gossip of the locals. They *all* had that information, but only Rahab believed and acted on that belief. This act of faith put her at odds with all the others but at peace with God.

EXPERIENCE GOD'S HEART

- *How did you learn about Jesus before you put your faith in him?*

- *When you first shared your faith in Jesus with other people, how did they receive you?*

- *Has your loyalty to Jesus been tested? If so, how?*

Faith Saves

We must remember that Rahab had the spies utterly at her mercy. She could have turned them out. She could have turned them in. In her home they were surrounded on every side by enemies. Their situation was precarious. They could not escape without her help. Thankfully, Rahab was glad to give it. Her faith was in the Lord of Israel. She proved it by sheltering these defenseless men.

While she saved them, she asked them to save her. She realized that she was in just as precarious a situation. If Israel was about to wipe out Jericho, what would become of her and those she loved? How would they escape?

- *What concessions did Rahab request in exchange for protecting the spies (Joshua 2:12–14)? Did they agree to her terms?*

- *What further step did Rahab take to help them escape? What advice did she give them (vv. 15–16)?*

- *What additional demands did the spies make of Rahab to ensure her safety when Israel invaded Jericho? What did she do after they escaped (vv. 17–21)?*

- *Does this demand remind you of another time God miraculously rescued people by a sign marking the outside of their homes (Exodus 12:21–23)?*

In exchange for her help, Rahab asked the men to spare her when they came back to attack Jericho. They readily agreed. But they were still inside a city of enemies. To keep their promise, they had to escape. So Rahab lowered them from her window with a bright red rope.

As they rappelled down the city wall, trusting their lives to the rope, the spies realized a future dilemma. In the mayhem of a military attack, they might mistake Rahab and her family for enemies and inadvertently break their vow of protection. How could the Israelite army know whom to protect?

The solution was literally slipping through their hands. The red cord that saved them could also save Rahab and her family.

This rope they clung to could be hung from the window to identify Rahab's house. It would become the lifeline for them all.[8]

As the spies scurried away to hide, Rahab did as she promised. Based on what she knew, she stepped forward in faith to serve the Lord and join his covenant people by harboring their spies. This act of faith saved her. It is this faith that makes her a model for New Testament Christians.

- *What did the writer of Hebrews commend Rahab for doing in this story (Hebrews 11:31)? What was the result of her faith?*

- *Name some of the others listed in Hebrews 11. In your opinion, how does Rahab compare with them? Why is she on the same list?*

- *Why does James mention her in his practical letter to Christians (James 2:20–26)? What actions did he say proved her faith? What point was James making about faith and works? How does Rahab illustrate this?*

In Joshua 2, Rahab did not stop being a prostitute. She simply believed God. We can presume that after she was saved from destruction, she changed professions. But at this point, she was a sinner saved by grace through faith. She was saved because of her faith not her righteousness.

No one is saved by their own righteous deeds or their shortage of unrighteous ones. Scripture is clear: "There is no one who always does what is right, no, not even one! There is no one with true spiritual insight, and there is no one who seeks after God alone. All have deliberately wandered from God's ways. All have become depraved and unfit" (Romans 3:10–12).

We cannot impress God with our goodness or our lack of badness. We can never boast that we were good enough for God to save us. We can only be included in his salvation by his grace. "For by grace you have been saved by faith. Nothing you did could ever earn this salvation, for it was the love gift from God that brought us to Christ! So no one will ever be able to boast, for salvation is never a reward for good works or human striving" (Ephesians 2:8–9).

The ways that God saves people are as diverse as the people themselves, but all of them are saved by faith. Like Rahab, we are all sinners saved by grace. There is no other way.

When Rahab sent the spies safely away, she was already safe. She was already right with God and included in his covenant people. She believed God. She trusted God. Final salvation was only a matter of time. So she waited for that ultimate rescue from God.

- *Whose instructions did the spies follow to get safely back to Joshua (Joshua 2:22–23)?*

- *What did the spies report to Joshua? Why were they confident that Israel could conquer the land (v. 24)?*

 DIGGING DEEPER

Hebrews tells us that Rahab was saved by her faith when she welcomed the spies. Of course, it would be days or weeks before she was rescued from the Jericho destruction. So which was it? The answer is both.

We often think of being saved as something that has already happened when we first put our faith in Christ. Certainly, the Bible speaks about being saved that way, but there are two more aspects that we often ignore or overlook.

Biblical salvation can also mean the process by which various aspects of our lives are gradually changing to reflect our salvation. In this sense, each facet of our lives is being saved little by little. Sometimes this process of salvation is called *sanctification*.

Furthermore, the Bible frequently speaks of salvation as something yet to come. When the Lord returns in judgment and sets everything right, when his permanent rule is established and sin is done, we will be gloriously, finally, and completely saved.

Read the following New Testament passages about salvation. Consider which aspect of salvation each refers to. Write beside each verse "Saved" for those that speak of salvation as already accomplished. Write "Being Saved" beside the ones that speak of the sanctification process. Finally, write "Will Be Saved" beside the Scriptures that are about God's ultimate salvation yet to come.

Matthew 10:21–22 _____

Luke 7:48–50 _____

Acts 16:30–31 _____

Romans 5:9–10 _____

Romans 8:22–25 _____

Romans 13:11–12 _____

1 Corinthians 1:18 _____

2 Corinthians 2:14–16 _____

Ephesians 2:8–9 _____

Philippians 2:12–13 _____

1 Thessalonians 5:8–9 _____

Titus 3:5–6 _____

Hebrews 9:28 _____

1 Peter 1:5 _____

Rahab's Legacy

Rahab of Jericho is mentioned unexpectedly in one other passage of Scripture. We find her name in another list at the beginning of the New Testament.

- *Why is Rahab listed in Matthew 1:5? Whose great-grandmother was she? Whose genealogy is she a part of?*

When Rahab believed and acted on faith, everything changed. Her relationships changed, and so did her destiny. Through the lifeline of that red cord, she became part of the bloodline of the Savior. This Rahab, a pagan sinner who was born the enemy of God's people, became an ancestor of God's Messiah through her risky act of faith.

⟨⟨♥⟩⟩ EXPERIENCE GOD'S HEART

- *Every believer has a coming-to-faith story. We sometimes refer to these as our personal testimonies. Think about your own. At what stage in the journey are you? Have you already heard enough, seen enough, and understood enough to believe? Are you still thinking about putting your faith in Christ? Are you already safe with the Lord and growing in him? Recount where you are in relationship to God and how you got there.*

- *If you are already a follower of Christ, reflect on your personal testimony of faith. How is it unique to you? Now how is it like the stories of so many others? What do you have in common with all your brothers and sisters in Christ?*

♥ SHARE GOD'S HEART

- *Have you ever felt frustrated because you can't seem to share your faith in Jesus with someone you really care about? The opportunity to talk about Christ just hasn't come up. Is it any comfort to you to know that God has many creative ways to get his good news to them? Of course, this doesn't mean that we don't have the delightful duty to tell the gospel message. But does it help to know that there are other voices in their lives that God can use? Explain your answer.*

- *Your personal experience with God is so useful in sharing your faith. When you tell it to others, they can't argue with your story. We can say, like the man in John 9 who was challenged repeatedly to explain his faith, "All I know is that I was blind and now I can see for the first time in my life!" (John 9:25). If you have shared your faith in Christ, retell the story here or to someone you know who needs to hear it. All of us need encouragement from time to time to share the good news.*

Talking It Out

1. With your group, take turns telling your personal coming-to-faith in Christ stories. After each one, comment on the unique features of each other's experiences. When everyone has shared their testimony, reflect on the commonality of faith itself bringing you together in Christ.

2. Discuss how loyalty to Jesus has affected your relationships. Do you have strained or broken friendships because you follow Jesus? Is your extended family confused, frightened, or threatened by your new faith? Do your colleagues or classmates jeer at or belittle you when religion comes up? Where do you find relief from the hardships of following Christ?

LESSON 4

Crossover

(Joshua 3:1–5:12)

With a high-resolution camera in everyone's pocket these days, it is hard to believe that a century ago, an affordable, portable, personal camera didn't exist. We take photos for many reasons. To provide evidence, to tell a story, to share an experience with people far away, to memorialize many of life's milestones.

What if you couldn't take a photo? How would you memorialize these significant moments? An engraved silver platter, maybe? A meaningful purchase like a crystal vase, perhaps? A medal, a wedding ring, a family Bible, a diploma, a death mask, a gravestone? These things are enduring witnesses of fleeting experiences. Of course, they help the participants remember the event, but more than that, they become heirlooms to pass on to another generation. Decades or centuries later, the artifact still does its work, reminding the residents of the future about turning points in the past.

After centuries of waiting, the moment had arrived. Israel would finally arrive in their promised land. What was always in the future was about to be in the past. It would happen in a single day without any photographers to make a record. But God had a plan to memorialize this moment for generations to come. It was so effective that we are still talking about that moment "to this day."

Preparing for Crossover

After hearing the report of the spies, Joshua was confident that the conquest could begin. He led all the people to set up camp on the edge of the river close to the crossing point.

- *How long did Israel camp on the Jordan's edge before mobilizing again (Joshua 3:2–3)? What do you think the people might conclude after three days on the edge of a river at flood stage? Would they be more eager or less eager to cross over? Would they be confident or confused about Joshua leading them there?*

- *What was the cue they were supposed to watch for that would tell them when and where to move out (vv. 3–4)? Joshua made a point to mention that they had never come this way before. Was this a subtle reference to Israel's failure the first time they were meant to enter the promised land?*

- *What did Joshua promise Israel that they would experience together (v. 5)? Compare Joshua's promise to the Lord's promise in Exodus 3:19–20. How are they similar? How are they different?*

- *According to the Lord, what would the Israelites learn about Joshua from the miracle he was about to perform (Joshua 3:7)? What did Joshua say the people would learn from it (v. 10)?*

 WORD WEALTH

When Joshua promised the Israelites the Lord would do *amazing things*, he meant the same category of miracles that God had done through Moses in Egypt. This Hebrew word *pala* refers to things *altogether separate* from expected things, natural things, human things. It is often translated "wonders."

When the Lord told Abraham and Sarah that they would have a child in their old age, Sarah laughed at the very idea. The Lord replied with this word, "Is there anything too hard [too amazing, too wondrous, too supernatural] for me?" (Genesis 18:14 NIrV).

When God sent Moses to Egypt with a demand that the pharaoh free the Hebrew slaves, God promised that he would strike Egypt with wonders until the king of Egypt let his people go (Exodus 3:20). In the wilderness, God again promised Moses that he was just getting started. In the conquest of the promised land, they would see wonders like no nation before had ever seen (34:10).

On the edge of the Jordan, on the cusp of fulfillment, Joshua draws on these promises to encourage the people for the enormous task ahead of them. It was no natural job to be done. It was no human battle to be waged. God himself would do wonders for them, Joshua declared, so expect to experience him.

A Wondrous Crossover

• *Whose act of faith began the crossover? What surprising and dangerous thing did God tell them to do? What happened when they stepped into the river (Joshua 3:8–16)?*

• *In preparation for the crossover, how many men were to be chosen? Did Joshua tell them what God had chosen them to do (v. 12)?*

- *Do you see any similarities between this crossover and the miracle God performed at the Red Sea (Exodus 14:21–22)? What is new?*

- *How long did the priests stand in the river (Joshua 3:17)?*

At Joshua's command, the priests hoisted the ark onto their shoulders and marched toward the raging Jordan. The distance between them and the water shrank with each step, but the water continued to roar. It wasn't until the feet of those faithful priests touched the water that God performed his wonder. At that moment, the surging stopped. An invisible miracle dam blocked the flow of that river several miles away. The pressure diminished. The water drained away, and dry ground began to appear.

When the water stopped upstream from the priests, there was no single path through the river like there would have been at the Red Sea. All the riverbed downstream from Adam was open to cross, so the crossing could happen relatively quickly. We should not think of a long queue snaking across the Jordan but a mass of people moving from one bank of the Jordan to the other.

Monument to the Crossover

Once all the people were across, God put into action his plan for a memorial. He wanted this moment in their nation's history to be remembered. Joshua called the twelve men he had chosen by the tribes (Joshua 3:12) and gave them their simple and profound assignment.

- *What task of strength did Joshua ask the twelve men to perform (4:1–9, 19–24)? In a land full of rocks, why would these stones be significant?*[9]

- *What question were the river stones expected to prompt from future generations of Israelites (vv. 6, 21)?*

- *What answer should be given (vv. 7, 22–24)? Note the centrality of the Lord in the answer.*

• *Why did the Lord perform this miracle for Israel (v. 24)?*

• *How long would the Israelites be talking about this historical turning point for their nation (v. 7)?*

Representing the twelve tribes of Israel who crossed the Jordan, twelve men carried twelve stones from the dry riverbed. These stones became a monument to this historic intervention of God. Whenever their descendants asked about these stones, this silent rockpile could tell and retell the story of the crossover.

 DIGGING DEEPER

Flanked by embassies, the National Gallery, and the Church of St. Martin-in-the-Fields is Trafalgar Square. Built to commemorate the British naval victory over French and Spanish fleets, it contains a wide variety of memorials. Looking in any direction, a visitor sees busts, statues, and plinths of military figures, political leaders, and nobility. Most imposing is the 218-foot-tall column guarded by four sculpted lions and dedicated to the memory of Admiral Horatio Nelson, the hero and a casualty of the Battle of

Trafalgar. It is impossible to visit this square without being confronted with British history.

Other monuments and memorials achieve the same goal. A stroll through Gettysburg, Arlington, or Flanders Field Cemetery will evoke the sacrifice and courage of those soldiers lost there. The Pudding Lane monument recalls the London fire. We can still "Remember the Alamo" because of the restoration of the mission complex in San Antonio. And the magnificent Arc de Triomphe is an enduring tribute to the French Revolution and Napoleonic Wars. All these sites are attempts to keep the minds of the present reflecting on the exploits of the past.

In the Bible, there are many such monuments scattered about the Holy Land. Whether a rockpile, a tomb, an altar, or a pillar, each is a physical landmark for spiritual landmark moments. Usually, the memorial pays tribute to a turning point in the life of a believer.

- *Read about these monuments and make note of who built them and what event and lesson they were meant to recall. You will need to read the surrounding verses to gain the context for each memorial so you can complete the chart.*

Scripture	Builder	Event	Lesson
Genesis 28:18			
Genesis 31:51–52			
Genesis 33:20			

Genesis 35:7			
Exodus 17:15			
Exodus 24:4			
Judges 6:24			
Isaiah 56:5			

Completing the Crossing

- *Who were the first people into the riverbed and the last out (Joshua 4:10–11, 15–18)? Why should they start and finish the process?*

- *What Israelites are specifically mentioned in the crossing (4:12–13)? Why were they mentioned here? Review Joshua 1:12–15.*

After the priests had taken the memorial stones out of the riverbed and the whole nation had crossed over, the priests came out of the Jordan. The priests were the key to this miracle. Their leadership and faith were instrumental in the crossover. Their presence in the riverbed held back the current. The flow of the river stopped and started with them.

Every Israelite had to pass by priests holding the ark of the covenant. The twelve men took their stones from near where the priests stood. The visible role that the priests played in the crossover proved the centrality of the Lord in this miracle. It reminded the people before, during, and after the crossover that they were God's people. Moses was his prophet and Joshua was their commander, but it was the Lord who led Israel.

As soon as the priests stepped onto Canaan's bank, the river flowed again. The raging flood-stage river that had been in front of them was now behind them. God had done it! That barrier was no barrier to the Lord. He brought them through, and there was no going back. Even if they panicked and turned around, they couldn't go back. The river that had kept them out of the promised land now kept them in. That crossing was a one-way trip.

- *How did this miracle affect the way that the Israelites viewed Joshua as their leader (3:7; 4:14)?*

- *What effect did this miracle have on the local kings of the Amorites and Canaanites (5:1)?*

The psychological impact of the crossover on Israel and the residents of Canaan were profound. Israel recognized the Lord's power and anointing on Joshua. Because he was leading them through water on dry ground just like Moses did at the Red Sea, they esteemed him just like they had Moses.

The Canaanites also recognized the power of God in this miracle. They knew the power of the Jordan River, but the Lord proved more powerful. If the awe-inspiring natural world was no match for him, how would they stand against him or his people? The fight went out of them. They knew their future was in jeopardy.

Leaving the Desert Behind

It is a good thing that the local chiefs were intimidated by Israel at this point because what God demanded next made Israel incapable of battle for a while.

- *What religious ritual did the Lord command Joshua to carry out when they entered the promised land (5:2–3)? Does this make strategic sense to you? Why do you think God waited to insist on this until they were on the Canaanites' side of the river?*

- *Why did all the men of Israel need to submit to this ritual (vv. 4–8)? How long did they wait until moving on?*

- *What was the spiritual result of this nationwide step of obedience (v. 9)?*

- *What religious holiday did the Israelites celebrate after the crossover (v. 10)? What events did this annual feast commemorate (Exodus 12:12–14)?*

- *Why are these two religious rituals mentioned together (Exodus 12:48)?*

- *What did the Israelites do in Canaan that they could not always do during their time in the wilderness (Joshua 5:11)? Because food was now readily available to them, what miracle ceased that day (v. 12)?*

Safely on Canaan's side of the river, the people of Israel paused to re-establish two ceremonies. In the forty years since Egypt, they had not circumcised their boys. Only the Egypt generation had this outward physical marking of covenant with God. That generation was outwardly in compliance, but their hearts were not with the Lord. Over and over, they stubbornly rebelled against God's leadership and complained about his care.

Their obstinance was most obvious the last time Israel was on the verge of entering the promised land. They openly rejected the guidance of God and refused to take the inheritance he offered them. So all those outwardly compliant rebels died in the wilderness.

Now there was a generation of Israelites who were inwardly compliant. They followed the Lord's leadership. They obeyed his command to go in. They crossed over. But they were lacking the outward sign that the Lord required. These circumcisions settled this problem. The shame of the disobedient Egypt generation was over.

Rededicated, they celebrated their Passover in the new land, remembering their deliverance from slavery in Egypt. Even their food changed in Canaan. From Gilgal, a new generation could go forward in obedience.

More Enduring Than Stone

The rockpile at Gilgal is gone. At some point over the centuries, the stones were scavenged to build a wall or a shelter. But it was there when the history of Joshua was recorded. We know this from the phrase "to this day" found in Joshua 4:9. The crossover participants thought it would always be there. They couldn't imagine something more enduring than stone. And yet.

We still remember the crossover. We still talk about it and pass the story along to our children. We have something more enduring than stone. We have the written history of Scripture, inspired by the Holy Spirit, to continue teaching and reminding us of this turning point moment in the history of faith. Because of Scripture, we confidently declare the same truths the people of God learned that day. The Lord who made the promise can keep the promise. He split the Red Sea; he stopped the Jordan River. A God like that is powerful. A God like that is awesome. No obstacle, physical or spiritual, can keep him from carrying out his plans.

 EXPERIENCE GOD'S HEART

- *Think about a "crossover" moment, when a life event and the spiritual lessons you learned from it changed your life forever. Some momentous event like the birth of a child, the move to a new region, victory over an addiction, or the death of a spouse. What did the experience teach you about the Lord? Thank him for revealing himself to you.*

- *Do you have any spiritual keepsakes, items passed down to you that teach lessons about the Lord's faithfulness? If you haven't looked at that item in a while, dig it out and rehearse what you learned about God at that point in your life.*

⚡ SHARE GOD'S HEART

- *Children love to hear and tell stories. In fact, they can absorb a complex idea better if they hear it in a story. Tell a personal faith story to a child in your life. Let them ask questions and take the time to answer them.*

- *It wouldn't have done much good for Israel to bury their rockpile in a hole. The same is true of your spiritual mementos. If you have any hidden away in a box in the attic, consider taking them down and placing them around your home. Put the items in obvious places. You could call attention to them or see if people inquire about them. When they do, there's a God-given moment to share your faith.*

Talking It Out

1. As you prepare to meet with your small group or Bible study partner, find a family heirloom that tells a story. Hopefully, it will be an object that is *very* old. The fact that you still have it is testament to its meaningfulness. What do you know about it? Who made it? Why do you have it? Tell this story to the group.

2. Jesus gave Christians some portable rockpiles, tangible reminders of momentous events. Wherever there is water, a new believer can be baptized. Discuss how baptism is like the crossover of Israel. Wherever there is bread and wine, believers can graphically remember the death, burial, and resurrection of Jesus on our behalf. Talk about how communion is like a memorial. If you wish, the group could share communion together and remember Jesus.

LESSON 5

All Around the Town

(Joshua 5:13–6:27)

Familiarity breeds inattention. Familiar songs can roll off the tongue on autopilot without giving any thought to the words. Think of all the times you have sung the amazing truths of the hymn *Amazing Grace* without concentrating. Familiar living space can blind you to maintenance or upkeep issues. Think of the times you have noticed an exposed wire or unfinished painting or clutter in *someone else's* house, but you have gotten used to looking at your own property uncritically.

The same thing happens with familiar stories. Think of nursery rhymes. You have heard them so often and said them so instinctively that it doesn't even bother you that there's a rock-a-bye baby falling out of a tree. Or a child in the corner eating his Christmas pie with his grubby little hands. You don't question living in a pumpkin shell. You probably aren't troubled by that peeping Tom, Willie Winkie. And you don't know what a *tuffet* is. These words are so familiar that we don't think carefully about them.

"Joshua Fit the Battle of Jericho" suffers from the same problem. Along with Noah's Ark, David and Goliath, Jonah and the Whale, and Daniel in the Lions' Den, this story is more than a little familiar. Familiarity breeds inattention. We have sung it, read it, and maybe even painted it on the nursery wall. It is a tale so familiar that we miss the details, or worse, we miss the point.

Before you read on, pray that God will help you notice

something new and unexpected in this well-worn story. Pray for Spirit-prompted attention to hear, understand, and apply this new lesson.

Surprising Strategy

The first obstacle to taking the promised land was the imposing fortress of Jericho. Archaeologists have learned much about this city through decades of excavations. While Jericho was not a large city, it was very well-fortified. The whole city was built on an eight-acre mound and is probably the oldest city in the region. It was protected by two parallel thirty-foot-tall walls, an inner wall eleven to twelve feet thick and an outer wall six feet thick built on the edge of the mound.

We can think of Jericho as a garrison city, built purposely over the centuries to repel an attack. If Jericho could not be breached, it would remain a rallying point for Canaanite soldiers. If Jericho did not fall, there would be little hope of conquering the whole land.

Jericho was where the spies hid out at Rahab's home inside the city's inner wall. Now that the whole nation had crossed the Jordan, the rest of the Jericho account unfolded as Joshua took a lonely walk in the shadow of the walls of Jericho.

- *Describe the unusual person that Joshua met (Joshua 5:13–15). What physical details and what titles does Scripture use to describe him?*

- *When he saw this impressive swordsman, Joshua wanted to know something. (This was probably a question any soldier would ask any stranger.) What was it (v. 13)?*

- *Did Joshua get a satisfying answer (v. 14)? What did he realize about this man? How did he respond to that realization?*

- *What did the swordsman command (v. 15)? How did this compare to Moses' first encounter with Yahweh (Exodus 3:1–6)?*

This stranger brushed aside Joshua's first question. Joshua asked an either/or question, but the answer was neither. In an instant, Joshua recognized that the only question that mattered was whose side was allied with the army of the Lord. He wanted his army to be on the Lord's side.

This mysterious figure was obviously divine since he received Joshua's immediate reverence and obedience. Joshua offered no objections, but instead he listened attentively to every instruction.

Even the most eccentric military planner could never have dreamed up the surprising strategy God dictated to Joshua. It wasn't a natural or logical way to wage war. However, for the leader who recently walked his nation through the Jordan River on dry ground, anything was possible.

- *What precautions was Jericho taking against the Israelites camped nearby (Joshua 6:1)?*

- *Look for details in the Lord's plan for taking Jericho (vv. 2–9). What were the Israelites to do each day? Who would be marching?*

- *Who would be at the front? What items were the leaders to carry? What sounds would be heard as they marched? How many circles did the Israelites make around the city? When were the soldiers to take up weapons?*

- *What did Joshua forbid the army to do as they marched (vv. 10–14)? How many days did the soldiers take this seemingly passive walk around the city?*

- *Imagine yourself a resident of Jericho. Would this strategy have confused, amused, or frightened you? Imagine yourself as a soldier in the Israelite army. Would this strategy have given you confidence or concern?*

The notions of battle, conquest, destruction, and victory all suggest heroic action. Soldiers, commanders, and armies take action. In any battle plan, we expect initiation and aggression. Not so at Jericho. Picture all the fighting men rising early, lining up, taking a short walk, and retiring back to their campsites. That was it! That was the plan. For six days, that is all these men of action were allowed to do. What restraint they showed to follow God's directions.

This calm, passive tactic was not their idea. It was not the brilliant scheme of military advisors and battle tacticians. This was God's plan for their first conflict in the promised land. Why such a surprising start to this military campaign?

Any other approach might have misled Israel into believing their own prowess was the basis of victory. They might have credited the win to their own courage, their own cleverness, or their own strength. This God-ordained beginning thoroughly debunked those ideas. Israel would win at Jericho because of Yahweh and only Yahweh.

🕎 DIGGING DEEPER

When Moses found the Israelites worshiping the golden calf at the bottom of Mount Sinai, he asked an important question that echoes through Israel's history: "Who is on the LORD's side?" (Exodus 32:26 ESV). If you are, you win. If you are not, you lose.

No military, no matter how well-armed or well-trained, can stand against the Lord. At their most faith-filled moments, God's people have always known this. "If God has determined to stand with us, tell me, who then could ever stand against us?" Paul rhetorically asked the Romans (Romans 8:31).

Almost to prove this point, God inspired some exceedingly strange battle plans over the centuries. Because of their outlandish methods, these battles could in no way be construed as human victories. As with Jericho, only God would plan such strategies, and only God deserves the credit for these wins.

- *Read about some of these instances. Then draw lines connecting the divine victory with the correct Scripture passage and the right personality.*

Judges 7:17–23	Victory because an old man kept his arms in the air	Elisha
2 Kings 6:14–23	A tiny squadron routed a vast army with jugs, horns, and torches	Joshua
Exodus 17:8–16	Overcame an armed warrior and his side-kick with a slingshot	Jehoshaphat
2 Kings 19:14–19, 32–36	Destroyed an army with praise songs	Hezekiah
2 Chronicles 20:2–28	Prophet supported by an invisible army	David
1 Samuel 17:41–50	One angel wipes out an empire's army	Gideon

It was the Lord who freed the Israelites from Egypt, who fed them in the wilderness, who dried up the waters for them to cross. And it would be the Lord who won the battle at Jericho. He alone would be their champion and victor. The New Testament tells us that Israel showed admirable faith when they cooperated with this strategy for victory at Jericho (Hebrews 11:30). The dependent and grateful attitude instilled at Jericho was meant to be the pattern for the whole conquest.

Many years later, a Hebrew bard would put this spiritual outlook to song: "Some find their strength in their weapons and wisdom, but my miracle-deliverance can never be won by men. Our boast is in Yahweh our God, who makes us strong and gives us victory!" (Psalm 20:7).

THE BACKSTORY

The Joshua account of the fall of Jericho has inspired archaeologists for centuries. If such a victory really occurred, surely archaeological evidence would confirm it. No one doubts that Jericho's "walls came a-tumblin' down." It is only a matter of when and how. Sceptics blame an earthquake. Some mechanical engineers suggest it was pulse dynamics that led to the crumbling of the ramparts.[10] Believers call it a miracle.

The earliest excavations at Jericho seemed to confirm almost every detail of the Bible record. Particularly, the work of John Garstang in the 1930s provided a wealth of evidence to bolster Jewish and Christian confidence in Scripture. However, "these finds and the interpretation given them were not satisfactory to some, for they could find no place in their thinking for a Jericho which so closely conformed to the biblical record."[11]

After her painstaking excavations in the 1950s, the British archaeologist Kathleen Kenyon concluded that the ruins were from the wrong historical era to be the Jericho of Joshua 5–6.[12] Many sceptics were relieved at her assessment. As a result, the Bible story has often been interpreted as a just-so story to explain the physical ruins of Jericho that the Israelites stumbled upon when they crossed into Canaan.

Dozens of articles and books have taken this view of the biblical account, some of them casting doubt and derision on the whole Israelite invasion. One such sample appeared recently in *Time* magazine and concluded that in the era when the Israelites arrived, "the wall of Jericho began its slow metamorphosis from a thing of stone and earth into an object of pure myth. A remarkable victory, it might be said, given that the Israelites probably never conquered Jericho at all."[13]

However, not all current archaeologists take such a jaundiced view of the Bible. Some have looked at the data and drawn the opposite conclusion. For example, Bryant Wood, a specialist in Canaanite pottery of the Late Bronze Age wrote:

> Jericho was once thought to be a 'Bible problem' because of the seeming disagreement between archaeology and the Bible. When the archaeology is correctly interpreted, however, the opposite is the case. The archaeological evidence supports the historical accuracy of the biblical account in every detail. Every aspect of the story that could possibly be verified by the findings of archaeology is, in fact, verified.[14]

Even those who doubt the historicity of the biblical account have observed many corroborating facts. Jericho was strongly fortified, its destruction occurred just after harvest time in the spring, the inhabitants had no opportunity to flee with their food-stuffs, the attack was swift, the walls were leveled, but possibly by an earthquake, and the city was not plundered but was burned instead.[15] Every one of these facts is in keeping with the biblical account of Joshua.[16]

Thirteenth Time's a Charm

For six days the ark and the fighting men made one loop, but the battle plan for the seventh day was different. This 6:1 ratio was long-established in Israel by now. The Sabbath, which God set apart since the week of creation, was an explicit ritual in the Feast of Unleavened Bread (Exodus 12:15–16) and the gathering of Manna (16:21–30). Then at Sinai, it became a lasting command for the Israelites in the Ten Commandments (20:8–11).

So at Jericho, the covenant patterns continued. After the ritual circumcisions and the Passover feast, the Israelites' first exploit included a Sabbath victory.

- *What were the marching orders for Day Seven (Joshua 6:15–16)?*

- *What did Joshua tell them to do after the final lap of Jericho (v. 16)?*

- *What did he warn them not to do? Why (vv. 17–19)? What exception did Joshua make (v. 18)?*

- *After the marching, the trumpet blasting, and the shouting, what happened to the strong defensive walls of Jericho (v. 20)? What did this allow the Israelite warriors to do (vv. 20–21)?*

- *After the battle, what prophecy did Joshua make about the ruins of Jericho (v. 26)? How did this prophecy eventually come to pass (1 Kings 16:34)?*

- *Why do you think Joshua wanted Jericho to remain a ruin?*

Rahab's Rescue

Just as the Jericho story started in Rahab's home, so the Jericho battle ends there. While the rest of the city was destroyed, the promises made to Rahab in Joshua 2:14 were kept. God's salvation finally and fully came to the one ally of Israel in the city.

- *Whom did Joshua send to safely escort Rahab and her family out of the doomed city (6:22–23)? In all the ruckus, how did they know how to find her (2:18)?*

- *As we learned in chapter 3, Rahab lives among us "to this day" (6:25). What is Rahab's lasting physical legacy to Christians (Matthew 1:1, 5)?*

• *List all the other survivors of Jericho (Joshua 6:21–25).*

• *What happened to all the other occupants of the city? What about the city itself? What did the people of the Lord do with all the valuable metals they found there (v. 24)?*

That day Rahab and her family joined the people of God because of her faith in the Lord and her faith-prompted rescue of the spies. She rescued them, and now they rescued her. Even in all that judgment and destruction, God's heart was eager to save.

Jericho had fallen! The first victory of the conquest was the oldest and most formidable city in the promised land. The Lord proved that he would keep his promise to give Israel a home. God showed them that they could expect complete victory if they cooperated fully with him. Going forward, they could be strong and courageous, trusting his mighty strength to accomplish the mission.

EXPERIENCE GOD'S HEART

• *Did God answer your prayer at the beginning of this lesson? Did you learn anything new from the battle of Jericho? Is there any specific idea the Lord taught you this time? Write it down.*

• *Isn't the creativity of God amazing? Who would have thought that walking in circles would topple defensive walls? Has the Lord ever done something in your life in an unconventional way? Did he use someone unexpected to point you in his direction? Did he use a terrible hardship to do a magnificent good in your life? Record what happened and what you learned from it.*

- *For an enjoyable diversion, watch this barbershop-style choral performance of "Joshua Fit the Battle of Jericho." The musical and visual storytelling elements are delightful: https://binged.it/3wqQKdT.*

 SHARE GOD'S HEART

- *An unstoppable God with good plans in store for his people is a good God to pray to. So ask three friends to tell you three things they need prayer for. (It might surprise you to learn that even atheists will usually answer this question.) With those nine items in mind and the confidence in a wall-toppling God, pray about those things for thirty days. Keep notes on what happens next.*

- *As you pray for the non-believers in your life, look for obvious cracks in their defensive walls. Remember, no obstacle can keep the Lord out if he means to get in.*

Talking It Out

1. Read together about Joshua's encounter with the mysterious swordsman. Why do we usually want to know which side the swordsman is on? Talk about how any group of people can know whether they are on the Lord's side.

2. If you have any military or former military personnel in your group, ask them to talk about God's strategy at Jericho. How would soldiers have felt during most of the Jericho operations? Have you ever felt like you were walking around in circles during your deployments? Did your assignment ever seem nonsensical only to turn out to be exactly the right strategy?

LESSON 6

Stolen Treasure

(Joshua 7–8)

A gentle trickle did its work. The secret drip, drip, drip of water saturated and dissolved more than four thousand tons of limestone. This process took hundreds, maybe thousands, of years, inexorably creating a massive subterranean cavern.

No one could have known the extent of the erosion when they built the 115,000-square foot National Corvette Museum on the surface in Bowling Green, Kentucky, in 1993. As builders erected its Skydome exhibit hall and its twelve-story spire, no one suspected. When they moved more than eighty valuable collectable sports cars into the finished space, no one guessed. When thousands of visitors toured the museum for almost ten years, no one knew.

But on the morning of February 12, 2014, everyone knew. Overnight, the concrete pad in the exhibit hall gave way beneath eight of those vintage Corvettes. Seconds later, they lay twisted and mutilated at the bottom of a sinkhole thirty feet deep. The damage to the cars alone (not to mention the facility) was estimated at over $1 million.

The tumult of that morning did not play out in public. The erosion was not on display like the cars themselves. It was secret, stealthy, and silent. Not even the staff at the Skydome knew what was happening directly beneath their feet. When they locked up that Tuesday night, they fully expected to carry on as usual the next day, but that secret activity changed everything.

Joshua 6 ends on a high point. The God of Israel led his people to a startling victory over the oldest and most well-fortified fortress in Canaan. Their first victory was total. The city was destroyed. Their enemies were killed. Their commander was instantly a famous and feared hero. If Jericho could fall so suddenly, so miraculously, then the conquest of the promised land was sure to be a complete success.

A Stunning Defeat

Then, suddenly, the devastating sinkhole appeared. Something happened in secret to undermine the progress of Israel as they moved on from Jericho. And on the heels of a stunning victory, a shocking defeat occurred in the hill country fifteen miles north of Jericho in the small town of Ai.

- *Recall the directions Joshua gave to the army as the walls were about to fall (Joshua 6:17–19).*

- *What violation happened at Jericho (7:1)? Who was responsible? Who knew about it?*

- *What did the scouts conclude about Ai, the next city Israel planned to conquer (vv. 2–3)?*

- *How did that campaign go (vv. 4–5)? Describe the casualties and the extent of the defeat.*

- *Compare Joshua 5:1 to 7:5. How did the tables turn and why?*

Perhaps, it is obvious with thirty-five hundred years of hindsight, that pride went before destruction at Ai (Proverbs 16:18). The scouts who went there were confident in their own military ability. They believed that with minimal force and a smidgen of pluck, they could take this small town. To them, it was simple math. With the still smoldering ruin of Jericho behind them, it seems they forgot where that victory really came from. Joshua agreed with them and sent his men to a humiliating defeat.

 DIGGING DEEPER

Be humble or be humbled. This biblical principle flows like a widening stream through Scripture. Pharaoh would not acknowledge the superiority of God (Exodus 10:3), so he was humiliated by the son of a slave woman. Nebuchadnezzar believed his own power and wisdom built his kingdom (Daniel 4:28–33), so he was brought low by insanity. Herod Antipas was raised to the status of deity by his audience (Acts 12:21–24), so the Lord cut him down.

Even God's friends face humiliation on occasion. Sarah needed to be called out for her unbelief (Genesis 18:10–15). Uzziah needed to learn his place (2 Chronicles 26:16–20). Isaiah needed to see how unclean he was in comparison to the holy God (Isaiah 6:1–6). Peter needed a rooster to rebuke him for his cockiness (Luke 22:54–62). Like Joshua at Ai, the Lord's people need to learn and relearn that dependence on God is the only posture for a life of faith.

In humility, our model is Jesus, of course. The Son of God, divine in nature, took on a servant's nature. The Maker was made human. The All-powerful became powerless, an infant in a maiden's arms. He did not come to be served but to serve. If that was not stooping down enough, he endured death, the ultimate in human defeat. Worse still, it was death by crucifixion, the most humiliating form of death (Philippians 2:5–11). Lower and lower until...

- *Complete these Bible verses about humility. Underline the consequences for the proud and circle the rewards for the humble.*

    Psalm 18:27: To the humble you bring _____,
but the proud and haughty you _____.

    Proverbs 3:34: If you _____ you will
learn to mock, but God's _____ flow to the meek.

Proverbs 11:2:   When you act with presumption, convinced that you're right, don't be surprised if _____! But humility leads to _____.

Isaiah 57:15 (NIV):   For this is what the high and exalted One says..."I live in a high and holy place, but also with the one who is _____ in spirit, to _____ of the lowly and to _____ of the contrite.

Matthew 23:12:   Remember this: If you have a lofty opinion of yourself and _____, you will be humbled. But if you have a modest opinion of yourself and _____, you will be honored.

James 4:6:   God _____when you are proud but continually _____when you are humble.

Philippians 2:8–9:   He humbled himself...Because of that obedience, God _____ and multiplied his greatness! He has now been given the _____!

Sobering Realization

This conquest could prove much, much more challenging than it seemed after the fall of Jericho. To the reader of this history, the cause of this defeat is obvious, but to Joshua and his leaders, it was mystifying. Had the Lord already abandoned them? Were their easy successes over? Would it be one hard slog of wins and losses from now on? Could they expect steady casualties like this from every minor outpost like Ai?

When you are full of questions like these, where do you find answers? When your doubts overwhelm you, where do you go? Joshua and Israel's elders turned to the Lord.

- *How did this defeat affect Joshua's confidence (Joshua 7:6–9)? What physical displays of grief and distress did he and the elders of Israel perform?*

- *By their reasoning, what missteps had they taken (v. 7)? What harm did Joshua suggest would come to the Lord himself (v. 9)?*

- *Was the Lord moved by Joshua's display (v. 10)?*

- *The Lord scolded the people for their prayers and intercessions. What did God reveal as the cause of this military defeat (vv. 11–12)?*

Secret Sin

- *Outline the plan the Lord had for revealing the secret sinner (vv. 13–16).*

- *What would the consequence be if they obeyed this plan? What do you think the consequence would have been if they had not?*

- *What items had Achan stolen from the plunder at Jericho (vv. 18–23)? Did Achan tell the truth? How does telling the truth give glory to God (v. 19)?*

- *The consequences of this sin against the Lord were terrible. List the items and individuals that were destroyed by stoning and fire (vv. 24–26).*

- *Does this punishment seem like too great a consequence for the sin described in 7:1? Why or why not?*

Achan believed his disobedience was a small thing. Jericho was a great fortress full of resources. What if only 99.9 percent of it was devoted to the Lord? What could his little salvage operation hurt? He thought he could hide this theft away where no one would see, safely bury it underneath his tent. No one else would miss his secret hoard, and no one would discover it. But like water dissolving limestone beneath the surface, his sin was doing its devastating work.

> Thus the passage underlines the awful effects of sin (see Rom. 3:9–20; 5:11–14). Because of one person's transgression, the occupation of the Promised Land is delayed indefinitely and many lives are lost in the process. Who can say what would have happened had Achan not sinned? Perhaps the battle at Ai could have been Israel's last. The other nations of Canaan would have

> responded like Rahab (and the Gibeonites) with belief in the one God of Israel, and Israel would have completely occupied the land. It is only with these verses that the reader of Joshua begins to realize the consequences of Achan's sin. The following chapters introduce the transition from a victorious people of God whose occupation of the land could have been the relatively simple matter of defeating those already discouraged to an unending history of battle, bloodshed, and idolatry that would haunt Israel throughout its history. As in the opening chapters of Genesis, so also in the opening chapters of Israel's dwelling in the Promised Land, a single transgression has cosmic ramifications.[17]

Achan did not factor in the omniscience of the Lord. Because of God's all-knowing nature, Achan's sin was never a true secret. Even as Achan scooped up those treasures from the doomed city, stashed them in his satchel, and slunk back to his tent to conceal them, the Lord saw what he was doing. So this process of discovery was a foregone conclusion. God and Achan knew the truth the whole time.

Achan followed the same order in his sin as Adam and Eve: he saw, he wanted, and he took (see Genesis 3:6; Colossians 3:5; James 1:14–15). This is in the heart of sinful creation in rebellion against the goodness of God's generosity and holiness. Similarly, Achan sought to hide himself (he did not come forward but required Yahweh to expose him). It is significant that the family of Achan was condemned for his sin in the same fashion that the descendants of Adam are condemned for Adam's sin.[18]

Sin always has deep and extensive costs that we do not consider and cannot anticipate. Did Ananias and Sapphira know that their faux generosity would put them in their graves (Acts 5:1–10)? Did David know that his adultery and its coverup would bring instability to his kingdom and violence into his own family (2 Samuel 12:1–12)? Did Adam and Eve know that their sin would plunge all their descendants into shame, suffering, and death (Genesis 3:8–19)? An awareness of potential consequences might discourage us from sinning.

THE EXTRA MILE

Nothing we do is a secret from God. The Lord sees and knows what people are up to. Does this realization bring you comfort or dread? Probably a little of both. What a comfort to know that evil people may be quietly hatching evil plots or even carrying out evil deeds, but they are not escaping God's notice. So we can trust the Lord. But what a dread to know that sometimes we ourselves are those evil people. So we should fear the Lord too.

For Christians, the Lord's omniscience should not be a cause for dread. Of course, he sees our sins. That is why Jesus came to save us from them. His death on the cross for us paid the penalty for every sin. Those of us who are in Christ through faith are forgiven. Our sin is behind us. Our slates are clean. Knowing this, our response when we sin should not be dread of his judgment but confidence in his mercy. When we acknowledge our sins, we can be certain that he will forgive and restore us (1 John 1:8–9). At the same time, we should not sin so grace can abound.

- *Read what Paul says about how Christians should now live in regard to sin and summarize what he concludes (Romans 6:1–6, 12–14).*

- *Now look up the following verses and jot down how each of these truths might be reason to fear and trust the Lord.*

Passage	Why I should fear the Lord	Why I can trust the Lord
Psalm 19:7–13		
Psalm 33:13–15		
Psalm 44:20–21		
Psalm 90:8		
Psalm 139:1–6, 23–24		
Proverbs 5:21–23		
Proverbs 15:3		
Ecclesiastes 12:13–14		
Jeremiah 23:23–24		
Hebrews 4:12–16		

Subsequent Victory

- *With the trouble of Achan dealt with, what exhortation did God repeat to Joshua as he sent him back to Ai (Joshua 8:1)? When have we heard this instruction before?*

- *The Lord demanded that all the valuables of Jericho be devoted to him. Did he make the same stipulations about Ai (vv. 1–2)? What was different?*

- *After the sin and defeat, how did the second attempt on Ai turn out (vv. 3–29)? Describe the events.*

With renewed confidence, the Israelites returned to Ai. This time Joshua went with them and took the best warriors, ten times the force of the first attack. Joshua's clever ambush strategy was inspired by the Lord, and God's involvement in tactics and timing is clear throughout. Like Jericho, the forces at Ai crumbled before Israel's army.

Incidentally, the plunder from this battle was free for the taking. Had Achan been patient and trusted the Lord and obeyed his instructions, he could have walked away from this battle openly with armloads of treasure. More importantly, the whole community could have been spared the loss and trauma of this whole shameful episode.

Service of Renewal

- *After the first two battles and as soon as they had secured this region, what did Joshua do to lead the nation in worship of the Lord at Mount Ebal (vv. 30–31)?*

- *What two things did Joshua do to reinforce for the people the importance of the written words of God (vv. 32, 34–35)?*

- *Joshua followed through on instructions that Moses gave him in Deuteronomy 27:1–26. How was this recitation of the Law supposed to happen?*

With the victories at Jericho and Ai, a portion of the eastern edge of Canaan was under Israelite control. This territory provided a foothold for Israel to begin moving inland, first to the south and then to the north. In the hiatus before those campaigns began in earnest, the nation paused for a covenant renewal. There, on the mountains inside their new territory, Joshua carefully reproduced, reread, and recited the law of Moses.

As at Joshua's inauguration, the centrality of the book of the Law was reinforced in this ceremony. They could go forward together with certainty that the Lord had spoken. His expectations were spelled out. His principles were there to counsel all subsequent generations. Any success or failure would rest on how they responded to God's written revelation. Only obedience to the Lord's word would lead them to victory and protect them from secret sin.

EXPERIENCE GOD'S HEART

- *Many Christians are uncomfortable with the notion of fearing the Lord. In the light of this part of Joshua, how do you feel about fearing the Lord? What feels right about it? What feels uncomfortable to you?*

- *It is a good practice occasionally to do some introspection to uncover our sin. Set aside some time and ask the Lord to "examine me through and through; find out everything that may be hidden within me. Put me to the test and sift through all my anxious cares. See if there is any path of pain I'm walking on, and lead me back to your glorious, everlasting way" (Psalm 139:23–24). Then when he shows you your sin, confess it and repent.*

9 SHARE GOD'S HEART

- *Christians are often accused of being holier-than-thou. Self-righteousness can be a problem. Jesus reserved his harshest words for those who were righteous in their own eyes. In your interactions with others, be quick to address your own sins. Maybe even lead with that.*

- *The next time a scandal comes up in conversation, talk about it as sin. Was that sin offensive primarily because it was wrong or because of the other person's position? Was it a sin that all of us have committed at some point? Why do people of prominence risk so much to sin? What is the fallout of that sin on the rest of us? Keep such a perspective in mind as you go forward in your walk with God, with fellow believers, and anyone else in your circle of influence.*

Talking It Out

1. Talk about our tendency to hide our sin. Why do we hide from each other? Why do we pretend like we are upstanding when we're not? If we know that God saw Eve's teeth marks in the fruit and Achan's treasure trove under his tent, how should we relate to the Lord about our own sin?

2. If Achan had obeyed, so much would have occurred differently. Share a time or two in your own life where disobedience led to damaging consequences. Balance that out by telling about a time or two where your obedience to God brought you unexpected benefits.

LESSON 7

Tricked into Treaty

(Joshua 9)

Like a heavy blanket, fear settled over the whole land of Canaan. From person to person and village to village, the word spread that a great swarm of people had crossed the Jordan and that they were intent on taking the lands. Their God is powerful. He sent devastating plagues on mighty Egypt where they were slaves until the pharaoh relented and let them go. Egypt's gods were no help to them. Then their God opened the Red Sea so that they could escape through it. Nothing could stand in his way. They wiped out two kings on the other side of the river and they have already taken Jericho and Ai. They are unstoppable!

Such was the gossip of Canaan. Such was the dread of its inhabitants. This dread was always part of God's battle plan for Israel. He promised that he would overwhelm the minds of their enemies with fear to open up the lands for conquering. While Moses received the law from God at Sinai as Israel was still camped in the valley below, the Lord revealed this strategy: "My angel will go ahead of you and bring you into the land of the Amorites, Hittites, Perizzites, Canaanites, Hivites and Jebusites, and I will wipe them out...I will send my terror ahead of you and throw into confusion every nation you encounter. I will make all your enemies turn their backs and run" (Exodus 23:23, 27 NIV).

From the day that God gave Israel victory over King Sihon on the east side of the Jordan, he promised that the victory would continue to strike fear in the hearts of their enemies. "See, I have given into your hand Sihon the Amorite, king of Heshbon, and his country. Begin to take possession of it and engage him in battle. This very day I will begin to put the terror and fear of you on all the nations under heaven. They will hear reports of you and will tremble and be in anguish because of you" (Deuteronomy 2:24–25 NIV).

Two Tactics

Faced with such terror, the locals had to act. Their property, their families, and their lives were in terrible jeopardy. This perfectly reasonable dread provoked action. This dread convinced Rahab she should cooperate with the spies to connive against her own city. This dread initiated the next stage in Joshua's conquest.

- *As word spread about the defeats of Jericho and Ai, how did the occupants of the land respond (Joshua 9:1–2)?*

- *However, the Gibeonites took a different tack. What crafty approach did they use to attempt to escape destruction from the Israelites (vv. 3–13)?*

- *What reasons did they give for wanting to make a treaty of peace with Israel? Compare their reasons with 2:9–10. What miraculous Israelite moments were famous among the people of Canaan (9:9–10)?*

- *Name three "proofs" the Gibeonites offered to show they lived far away (9:4–5, 12–13).*

Most of the frightened inhabitants responded with aggression of their own. If these interlopers had come to fight, they would get a fight. And what a fight it would be! Instead of waiting for the Israelites to come and pick off their cities one-by-one as they had Jericho and Ai, these kings and their armies banded together. Surely, five cities could put up some serious resistance.

Without a Prayer

However, the leaders of Gibeon understood that resistance was futile. If the God of the Israelites was truly unstoppable, what hope could there possibly be in opposing him militarily? Instead, the Gibeonites settled on a devious plan to make peace with Israel. With props and costumes, they boldly and deceptively approached the leaders of Israel in their own camp.

- *Did their ruse achieve its purpose (vv. 14–15)? Were the Israelite leaders fooled? What assurance did the Israelites give that they would not attack the Gibeonites? How could Joshua have foiled this deception?*

An interrogation followed. A handful of pseudo-proofs did the trick, and in short order, they had forged a treaty of peace with Israel. Fooled by this scam, Israel signed away a portion of their promised land without a fight. Ironically, the leaders of Israel swore an oath in the name of the Lord that day, the same Lord they failed to consult about this treaty.

Clearly, Israel didn't learn the lesson of Ai. Their human judgment proved insufficient to assess the situation again. At Ai, they reasoned they did not need a large force to take the city. With Gibeon, they reasoned these strangers were from such a distant land that they were no threat. Both blunders were preventable. If their conquest was to succeed, they needed to learn to depend on the Lord. They needed to seek him for wisdom in decision-making, not just for winning military battles.

 DIGGING DEEPER

The threat to God's people was thorough. Sometimes it was aggressive and confrontational. Sometimes it was subtle and deceptive. Whether it was an all-out assault or a sneaky ploy, Israel's enemies did not want their campaign to succeed. They wanted to limit the Israelite advances or halt them altogether. The enemy alliance would stop the Israelite possession of the land if they could.

Joshua's warfare is instructive for Christians facing spiritual opposition. Sometimes that opposition is aggressive and confrontational, even violent. World persecution of Christians is on the increase. Intimidation, confinement, torture, and even death are daily risks for countless believers around the world. Even when the opposition is not physical, it can be hostile: speech codes, legal battles, and anti-proselytizing policies often make living out one's Christian convictions difficult; non-official opposition can be personally painful too. Most followers of Jesus have faced mockery, exclusion, and scorn from formerly close friends.

Spiritual opposition can also be insidious and cunning: peer pressure to abandon Christian principles; the quiet, unrelenting damage of intellectual skepticism; the popularity of current social theories and philosophies; crippling guilt over past decisions; the allure of moral compromise; spiritual discouragement over besetting sins; resentment over past wrongs against us; doubt stemming from long-unanswered prayer. These soul-eroding strategies have proven effective against Christians on numberless occasions.

Underneath all this antagonism is the real enemy of our souls. Satan is no illusion, no religious personification of evil. He is a real being and a genuine threat. After many millennia of experience, he is skillful in his tactics (Genesis 3:1–6). If aggression can stop us, he will use that (Revelation 12:17). If subtlety is more effective, he will use that (2 Corinthians 2:11; 11:3–4). He is vicious, he is thorough, and he is determined (1 Peter 5:8).

But he is ultimately defeated already. Jesus lived a life like ours, facing all the temptations and trials that human beings do, resisting temptation all the way (Matthew 4:1–11; 2 Corinthians 5:21; Hebrews 4:14–16). Dying the death we deserved, the Sinless One bore our sins for us. He paid the righteous penalty for all wrong-doing on the cross (Isaiah 53:4–6; 1 Peter 2:24). So in Christ we are victors over sin and death (Romans 8:31–39; 1 Corinthians 15:54–58; 1 John 5:4–5).

With this total victory in hand, Jesus leads his people in battle against spiritual enemies (Colossians 2:13–15). We are empowered to win this battle (Luke 10:18–20). His miraculous unstoppable power is working inside us for victory (Romans 8:11). He has given us the spiritual weapons we need to put up a fight (2 Corinthians 5:3–5; Ephesians 6:10–18). In his strength, we can even stand firm and watch the devil run away (James 4:7; 1 Peter 5:6–9). We can live fearlessly no matter what the opposition brings against us (Hebrews 2:14–15), because at the final battle we will be standing alongside the ultimate Victor as he finally and completely vanquishes our great foe (Revelation 20:9–10).

Deception Discovered

With the treaty in hand, the Gibeonites went away to their "very distant land" and the Israelites planned their next move. They didn't realize that their next move would be cleaning up their last move.

- *How did the Israelites learn that they were duped? How long did it take? How did the people of Israel feel about the treaty then? Why were they angry with the leadership (Joshua 9:16–18)?*

- *Did the leaders decide to abide by their peace treaty even though it was negotiated deceitfully? Why? What adjustments did they make to the terms (vv. 19–23)?*

- *In essence, Joshua asked the Gibeonites, "Wouldn't you rather die than be slaves" (vv. 22–23)? Why do you think Joshua was baffled by their priorities? Remember his own birthplace and background.*

Interestingly, the treaty with Gibeon reversed the typical pattern of conflict between Israel and its leaders. From Egypt to the Jordan and throughout their wilderness wanderings, the people grumbled against leaders who were faithful to God. The people were in the wrong, and their whining was sinful. In this case, the people grumbled against leaders who had blown it. The leaders had ceded territory away from them without a prayer.

An oath in the Lord's name was not something to be sloughed off. They were forbidden to take God's name in vain. If they wanted God's blessing, they could not use his name for convenience only. If they wanted to stay in the Lord's presence, they would have to keep this promise, even when it hurt (Psalm 15:4).

With the community grumbling about them, the leaders added a stipulation to their peace treaty. While they would spare Gibeonite lives, they would subject them to hardship. To stay in the land, the Gibeonites were condemned to be servants to Israel forever.

Frankly, Joshua could not conceive how a free people would submit to servitude. He was born a slave. His people were finally free and in their own land. He would die for such a privilege. The Gibeonites traded their freedom for survival. It seemed like a good deal to them, but it was baffling to Israel. Yet, true to his word, Joshua saved the Gibeonites from death, and they became a permanent part of Israel.

- *How is the answer the Gibeonites gave to Joshua a profession of faith in God (Joshua 9:24)? As a result, what commitment did they make to Israel going forward (v. 25)?*

- *What would have happened to the Gibeonites if they had not taken this approach (v. 26)?*

- *How did this agreement with the Gibeonites lead to future provision for Israelite worship of the true God (v. 27)?*

Permanent Presence

This ill-considered treaty was a setback for Israel. Their inheritance was diminished by the enclaves of these deceitful partners. At least part of the land could never be completely their own.

When we read further in Old Testament history, we see Gibeonites cropping up here and there. When David was hiding in the wilderness, defending himself against the pursuits of King Saul, one of his leading warriors was Ishmaiah the Gibeonite (1 Chronicles 12:1–4).

Later when he became king, David moved the tabernacle to Gibeon where it became the most important worship site in Israel (2 Chronicles 1:1–13). This was where the tabernacle was when Solomon asked the Lord for wisdom instead of riches and a long life. Hundreds of years later, their city played this key role in the worship of Israel, just as Joshua predicted.

The Gibeonites even drew on this treaty of peace and protection outside the book of Joshua. During Saul's reign, he scoured the area for foreigners and killed many Gibeonites. The Lord revealed this breach of the treaty to David who then negotiated with them to avenge these deaths (2 Samuel 21:1–9).

Gibeonites were last mentioned as part of the contingent of Israel returning to the land after exile in Babylon (Nehemiah 7:25). There were almost a hundred men who returned with the Israelites to reoccupy Jerusalem and rebuild the wall (3:6–7).

For Gibeon's part, this treaty was a triumph. While they were relegated to the role of servants, they were not killed or driven off their land like most of their neighbors. Instead, they were eventually folded into the community of Israel. Furthermore, as we will soon see, they could count on the protection of the Israelites and their invincible God.

 DIGGING DEEPER

The conquest had barely begun and already there were Canaanites living among the Israelites under their protection.

From Jericho, Rahab's extended family joined the Israelites. Now the Gibeonite cities made peace with them.

Every salvation story is unique, but there are several fascinating parallels between these two. Have a look at their stories of salvation and make a note of the similarities you see. The first answer has been supplied already.

Rahab	Similarity	Gibeonites
Joshua 2:9–11	Heard about the Lord already	Joshua 9:9–10
Joshua 2:2–3		Joshua 10:4
Joshua 2:4–5		Joshua 9:6
Joshua 2:14		Joshua 9:15
Joshua 2:17–21		Joshua 9:25
Joshua 6:25		Joshua 9:26; 10:6–7

EXPERIENCE GOD'S HEART

- *How do you make a big decision when you are uncertain of the facts? Is prayer your first instinct or your last resort? Why?*

- *When you pray, do you feel like the Lord gives you the wisdom you need when you need it? Expand on your answer.*

- *Read through the list of battle armor that every Christian has for fighting (Ephesians 6:10–18). Consider what each piece is meant to do and write that below. For example, faith is the shield that protects against deadly piercing demonic attacks.*

- *What have you learned overall from Ephesians about how to engage in spiritual warfare?*

 SHARE GOD'S HEART

- *Do you know someone who seems to be under serious spiritual attack? Is it subtle or blatant aggression they are dealing with? Paul wrote that believers could help one another in these situations by praying (Romans 15:30–31). Fight alongside them in prayer, taking some time to do that right now.*

Talking It Out

1. Discuss your experiences with spiritual warfare. What kind of tactics work best against you? Is an all-out frontal attack more effective than a subtle erosive approach?

2. How do you defend yourself?

3. Have Christian leaders let you down? Did they make some blunder or commit some sin that still frustrates you? Israel's leaders sure did at Gibeon! Somehow, the community recovered and went on together to win great victories. How can a Christian group recover and move forward after leaders foul things up?

LESSON 8

Cosmic Cooperation

(Joshua 10–12)

Christmas night in 1776, George Washington took a small contingent of troops to Trenton, New Jersey, where British forces had left their Hessian mercenary reinforcements to establish an outpost. Recent losses in New York and dwindling numbers due to expiring enlistments and desertion made for a dispirited Continental Army. With limited resources, a head-on battlefield confrontation might have gone badly for Washington. So his daring men boarded boats and crossed an icy Delaware River in the middle of the night. This sudden, unexpected attack caught the enemy still asleep in their barracks. The surprise ended in a resounding victory for Washington and raised the morale of the American colonial army.

Israel's defeat of Ai came only after Achan's disastrous sin and an embarrassing defeat. Joshua's next step was a misstep. The ill-considered peace treaty with the Gibeonites hurt Israel's morale, and they grumbled against their leaders. Joshua needed an unalloyed win. Just in time, a surprise attack and the supernatural help of the Lord of Hosts would give him a string of victories.

- *The fame of Joshua and Israel was spreading. In addition to their deliverance from Egypt and the defeat of the Transjordan kings Sihon and Og, what new facts were frightening the occupants of Canaan (Joshua 10:1)?*

- *Why did Gibeon's submission have an especially big impact (vv. 2–5)?*

- *How did this redirect the alliance's hostility (compare 9:2 to 10:4)? How did making peace with Israel change Gibeon's relationship with their neighbors?*

The loss of Gibeon and its sister cities was a tremendous blow to the other inhabitants of Canaan. Gibeon, being a key city with strong warriors, could have been a valuable ally in repelling the Israelite offensive. They might have even been positioned to lead such a defense. Instead, Gibeon defected to the enemy.

In retaliation for that disloyalty, the armies that had been amassing against Israel turned their aggression toward Gibeon. In response, the Gibeonites relied on their new treaty partner for help.

- *What obligations did Israel have toward Gibeon because of the peace treaty (10:6–8)? What special assurance did they have going into battle against these enemies?*

- *Describe the battle. What human battle tactics were employed to win this victory? What three miracles occurred during the battle? What cosmic cooperation did Joshua plead for to give them time to complete the victory (vv. 9–15)?*

- *What did the writer of this account conclude about the Lord's involvement (v. 14)?*

When Joshua received the distress call from Gibeon, he did what the treaty demanded. The army of the Lord responded with an all-night march and surprise attack. Startled and divinely confused, Israel's enemies beat a hasty retreat with Joshua's army on their heels. An astounding triumph was at hand!

Success was never truly in question. On the march, the Lord assured Joshua that his enemies would all fall before him. Israel's military strength was the least of the Amorite worries. As they fled for their lives, enormous hailstones fell from the sky. They were being stoned to death by the Lord. For these doomed warriors, the day couldn't end soon enough.

And it didn't. The Lord, who sent supernatural disasters on Egypt, again proved his sovereign power over nature itself. Joshua asked for a longer day to complete the victory, and amazingly, the Lord answered his prayer.

 THE EXTRA MILE

A kindly, gentle, smiling old man sitting on a throne. An impersonal bright, warm light emanating outward. Mercy without justice. Benevolence without discipline. Our modern concepts of God are safe, benign, even insipid.

Even when we think of Jesus Christ, we tend to place him surrounded by children, tenderly touching the sick, constrained on a cross, or helpless in a manger. There is precious little room in our mental construct for Jesus scolding his disciples, damning the

Pharisees, or beating merchants with a whip, let alone judging the nations. Our tame half-Jesus doesn't do justice to the actual Son of God.

In Scripture, we have a more multi-dimensional picture of the Lord. He is Love, of course, but he is also our Judge. He is Prince of Peace, of course, but he is also a Warrior. In fact, over two hundred fifty times, the Old Testament calls him the Lord of Hosts, the Commander of all the Angelic Armies of heaven. Without this broader conception of God, many Bible passages are incomprehensible.

In Joshua 10:14, we read, "It was the day Yahweh himself fought for Israel! There has never been a day like it before or since—a day when Yahweh obeyed the voice of a man!" There has never been a day *exactly* like it, but examples of the Warrior Lord fighting for his people are numerous.

- *Read the following passages. Make note of the context. (What is the story or song preceding or surrounding the verse?) Then write down a personal application. (What difference would it make in my life if I knew the Lord this way?)*

	Context	Personal Application
Exodus 14:25		
Exodus 15:3		
Deuteronomy 1:30		

Deuteronomy 3:22		
Deuteronomy 20:4		
Joshua 23:3		
Joshua 23:10		
2 Samuel 5:24		
2 Chronicles 20:29		
Nehemiah 4:20		
Psalm 24:8		
Psalm 35:1		

Isaiah 42:13		
Romans 16:20		
2 Thessalonians 1:7–8		
Revelation 19:11		

Overcoming Kings

While their armies were fleeing and fighting for their lives, the leaders who instigated this disaster scurried off to hide. This proved to be a bad strategy for them, even lethal.

- *What self-defeating move did the five southern kings make to protect themselves (Joshua 10:16–21)? How did it backfire?*

- *How did this cowardly attempt at self-preservation give Joshua an opportunity to demonstrate Israel's dominance over the whole region (vv. 22–27)?*

- *What familiar instruction did Joshua give to the Israelites as he prepared to vanquish the enemy kings (compare Joshua 10:25 to Deuteronomy 31:6–7, 23 and Joshua 1:6–9, 18)? How was this graphic public display meant to encourage Israel?*

Joshua was a ruler without a crown, a head of state without a state. Cowering inside the cave at Makkedah were five of his enemies, legitimate local authorities ruling over geographic territories. These established kings embodied Joshua's opposition. They also stood for swaths of land that were about to come under Israel's rule. Joshua's public triumph over these kings displayed for his leaders that the victory they hoped for was certain to materialize.

Christians can have the same confidence in our spiritual struggles. We have a Leader who battled temptation alongside us and won. He fights for us (Romans 8:31). With us (John 14:16–18). In us (1 John 4:4). He has overcome the world (John 16:33). Through him, we are more than conquerors (Romans 8:37). Satan, our chief enemy, will be crushed (16:20). So no matter how menacing our enemies may appear, we can confidently fight back knowing that we will overcome them (1 John 5:4).

- *After conquering the five kings and their armies on the battlefield at Gibeon, Joshua went to each of their cities and wiped them out (Joshua 10:28–43). Throughout this series of victories, what sentences and phrases indicate that their success was miraculous (vv. 30, 32, 42)?*

- *How successful was this southern campaign (v. 42)? Who gets the ultimate credit for this success?*

 DIGGING DEEPER

"Everything that breathed was slaughtered—as Yahweh, the God of Israel, had commanded" (Joshua 10:40).

For most modern readers, there is one aspect of the conquest that can be emotionally distressing. Many of us in Western civilization live in a time of peace with most of our physical needs provided and little threat of violence. Combine this with our Western framework for human rights, and we become deeply uncomfortable with killing, even of our mortal enemies. The violence in today's movies and video games has desensitized us but makes us squirm when we read it in the Bible. Knowing that so many Canaanites were killed in these campaigns is disturbing. Knowing that Joshua's army did it under the direction of God is more troubling still.

Spiritualizing the conquest makes it more palatable. Maybe if we think of it in terms of spiritual warfare only, we don't have to face the brutality of these battles. However, an honest reading of biblical history won't allow that. A dozen times in these two chapters, the writer boasts of the complete destruction of the land's inhabitants (10:19, 28, 30, 32–33, 35, 37, 39, 40; 11:11–12, 14, 21–22). There is no getting around it. The command to carry out this warfare was divine. Israel really did wipe out their enemies. The bloodshed was genuine and copious. Canaanite suffering was severe.

How can a Christian come to terms with this carnage?

First, we should recognize that our current sensibilities are very modern indeed. For most of human history, violence was a fact of life. Territorial disputes for resources were commonplace. Slights against one's honor, family feuds, and historic grudges were usually settled with violence. In recent history, deadly duels and bloody fisticuffs were the standard way to resolve conflicts. Moreover, we should remember that less than a century ago, the sophisticated and "civilized" fought world wars that led to tens of millions of deaths. We have fine-tuned our military technology to kill hundreds or thousands from far away with the push of a button. With nuclear weapons, we can eliminate millions. Standing in judgment over ancient biblical warfare is a bit rich.

Second, we need to distinguish the individual from the whole. Nations can do what individuals cannot. An individual shooting a stranger is murder. A soldier shooting a soldier in war is not. An individual confining another is kidnapping. A sheriff, even a Christian sheriff, jailing a criminal is not. Nations have legitimate power to carry out justice and to make war. Christian individuals have a responsibility to turn the other cheek, forgive our enemies, and do whatever we can to live at peace. Nations do not have that obligation.

Third, we must remember that this was God's righteous judgment on wicked people groups. When God promised Abraham the land of Canaan as an inheritance for his descendants, he did so in terms of judgment. He would eventually seize this territory from the current occupants and give it to Abraham's children, but not yet. The wickedness of the people hadn't reached its full measure. He would let them devolve further into their own violence and depravity for hundreds of years before he would bring judgment upon them (Genesis 15:12–16; Leviticus 18:24–28). In Joshua's military campaigns, God's justice was finally carried out against these societies.

Fourth, we need to acknowledge the protective value of these wars. If your child is under threat, it is justifiable to eradicate the threat. Allowing the inhabitants to remain would have introduced a perpetual threat to Israel's safety and security. The spiritual perils of living side-by-side with these people were extreme. Infamous for their sexual indulgence and pervasive idolatry, surviving Canaanites would have been a perpetual spiritual snare to the Israelites (Deuteronomy 12:29–31). In fact, this became precisely the problem after the piecemeal conquest of the land.

Fifth, these claims of total annihilation were rhetorical hyperbole, in reality. These boasts in the text appear to be something of a middle eastern victory formula wherein the conqueror announced the total obliteration of his enemies even when the slaughter was less than complete. In Joshua 15, there are people living in cities that were "totally destroyed" in Joshua 10.

Sixth and finally, there was mercy even in this judgment. Those who acknowledged Israel's God and submitted themselves to Israel's rule over them were allowed to live in peace alongside them. Rahab and the Gibeonites are two obvious examples. The law of Moses anticipated foreigners living among them (Leviticus 19:33–34) as upstanding citizens like Araunah the Jebusite (2 Samuel 24:18–25) and Uriah the Hittite (2 Samuel 11:6–13).[19]

Taking the North

- *When the northern cities heard about the defeat of those in the south, they joined forces to fight Israel (Joshua 11:1–5). How did the writer describe the size of their joint army (v. 4)?*

- *What promise did God make to Joshua about this threat? What specific instruction did God give Joshua about the spoils after the battle? Did Israel obey God's instructions this time (vv. 6–9)?*

With the southern region of Canaan largely subdued, the next phase of the conquest turned north. Again, the Israelites did not go spoiling for a fight. The fight came to them as the northern kings formed a massive alliance of warriors and war machines.

As before, God made a promise to deliver the enemies over to Israel, but he also made a counterintuitive demand. Typically, a victorious army would confiscate the weapons of their enemies as the spoils of battle. In this case, the Lord commanded Joshua to hamstring the horses and burn the chariots. Why? In the Law,

Moses warned future kings of Israel against amassing large numbers of horses (Deuteronomy 17:16). The thrust of this instruction was that God wanted Israel not to put their trust in horses, not to number them, not to build up a permanent war arsenal. The Lord was their defense, and as this passage proves, he is enough.

- *As with the campaign in the south, Israel defeated these peoples on the battlefield and then in their cities (Joshua 11:10–17). How was their treatment of Hazor, the capital city, similar to the way they conquered Jericho (vv. 10–11)? How thorough was Joshua's obedience in following the Lord's directives (v. 15)?*

- *The book of Joshua describes the conquest of Canaan in fewer than sixty verses, but how long did this process take (v. 18)?*

- *Only Gibeonites were spared in this process. Why did none of the other people want to make peace treaties with Israel (vv. 19–20)?*

One more cluster of enemies is mentioned in Joshua 11: the Anakites. They are an ethnic group distinct from the other Canaanites. Their threatening presence in the land was of special concern to the Israelites. Their intimidating appearance and reputation as warriors frightened Israel out of invading the land forty years previously (Numbers 13:27–29). The Anakites were giants, descendants of the Nephilim. They were so tall that the Israelites felt like grasshoppers next to them.

When Moses asked the question, "Who can stand up against the Anakites?" it was a rhetorical question (Deuteronomy 9:1–4 NIV). Still, he promised, the Lord was stronger than any of their enemies, and he could defeat them.

- *Did Joshua flinch from fighting these giant warriors (Joshua 11:21–22)? How successful was his campaign? Where did the Anakites remain after Joshua's war against them? Incidentally, there are some giants from these towns in later biblical history (1 Samuel 17:4–7; 1 Chronicles 20:4–8).*

- *What previous leader of Israel is mentioned six times in Joshua 11? What is the significance of his memory in this passage? How thoroughly did Israel obey his commandments? Why might this be surprising?*

The Defeated Foe

- *Joshua 12 is the recitation of the cities and kings that Israel had already defeated. Read this section as a review. See if you can remember any of the people or place names. Not all the inhabitants were subdued, but Israel had neutralized all the major pockets of resistance. Now Joshua could divide up the land among the tribes.*

- *How much of Israel was involved in these conquests (10:7, 15, 21, 24, 29, 31, 34, 36, 38, 43; 11:7)? What long-term benefits do you think this united engagement with their mission had?*

In obedience to Moses and the Lord, that generation of Israelites took the land of Canaan for themselves and their descendants. Every tribe that would inherit this land was part of the conquest and so were the fighting men of the Transjordan tribes who had already received their land. All of them fought together. All sacrificed together. All worshiped together. All could celebrate together. This sweeping success was a victory for all of God's covenant people.

The apostle Paul wrote to the Philippians from a jail cell. Despite their inauspicious beginnings, he had high hopes for that local church:

> Whatever happens, keep living your lives
> based on the reality of the gospel of Christ.
> Then when I come to see you, or hear good
> reports of you, I'll know that you stand
> united in one Spirit and one passion—
> celebrating together as conquerors in the
> faith of the gospel. And then you will never
> be shaken or intimidated by the opposition
> that rises up against us. Your courage
> will prove to be a sure sign from God of
> their coming destruction. For God has
> graciously given you the privilege not only
> to believe in Christ, but also to suffer for
> him. For you have been called by him to
> endure the conflict in the same way I have
> endured it—for you know I'm not giving
> up. (Philippians 1:27–30)

No matter what kind of spiritual challenges the Philippian Christians might face, they could conquer. Even the most daunting opponents would not intimidate them or cause them to back down. If they stood together in Holy Spirit unity, trusting the Lord, they would triumph. And we will too.

♥ EXPERIENCE GOD'S HEART

- *How does your concept of God compare to the God of Joshua in this passage? Is there room in your thinking for a heavenly Warrior who wreaks justice on evil and societies in rebellion against him? Is your understanding of the Lord too tame?*

- *From the safety of their offices, politicians and diplomats often send soldiers to war. The incarnation of the Son of God proves that our Lord is not like that. Jesus entered the battle with us and became the enemy's chief target. How does that knowledge help you in your struggle? How does it motivate you to pray?*

♥ SHARE GOD'S HEART

- *Jesus' final command to his disciples was "Make disciples of all nations" (Matthew 28:19). Every step outward that Christians take with the gospel, they extend the rule of Jesus. If you think of this as a tactical mission, it means taking new territory. How are you participating in Jesus' conquest?*

- *Paul asked his friends in Thessalonica to "Pray that God will rescue us from wicked and evil people, for not everyone believes the message." Pray for missionaries and evangelists you know as they strive to take new ground in the campaign of Jesus Christ.*

Talking It Out

1. When Israel fought these battles in Canaan, the tribes all fought together. No tribe was shirking or side-lined. Afterward, they all celebrated because they all participated. How can Christians fight their spiritual battles together, shoulder-to-shoulder?

2. What might lead some Christians to sit out the battles?

3. How do we know that we are winning the spiritual war?

LESSON 9

Dividing the Conquered

(Joshua 13–19)

Let's say you want to go from Weyburn to Speedy Creek. How would you get there? Let's ask a local.

"It will take you three-and-a-quarter to drive it, but it's a simple trip. The first half will be on the diagonal highway. Not much to see there, except for the occasional elevator. Oh, be careful not to miss your turn at Corinne or you'll end up in the Queen City. You'll spend the rest of the drive on the Number One. You'll pass Mac the Moose on your left just before the junction with the Prince Albert highway. When you pass Briercrest in another quarter of an hour, you might want to stop in at the SS at Caronport for a CB. Or if you have your sweetheart along with you, you could swing by Boharm for a coffee. Wink, wink. Keep heading west and you'll go through the alkali beds at Chaplin. Then about twenty minutes later the highway goes across Reed Lake at Morse. You're almost there. A little over half an hour later you'll be coming into town. You'll know it when you cross Swift Current Creek and you'll see the Canadian Tire and PetroCan on your right."

Most readers will be mystified by that accurate, though colorful explanation. The lingo, the landmarks, and the locations would be well-familiar to the people living in that swath of southern Saskatchewan in Canada, but no one else would have any idea. Describing a journey without a map is like that. Without local experience or visual reference, there's the occasional point of interest that might pique your curiosity, but it is not riveting. At best, the description is entertaining and at worst, tedious.

Map for the Generations

For seven chapters, Joshua reports on just such details. Scorpion pass, Beth Pelet, Irpeel, the Boulder of Bohan, Rabbith, Madmannah, and so on. Hundreds of towns. Dozens of landmarks. Most of these locations are never mentioned again in Scripture. Nearly all these places have different names now. Some of them don't even exist anymore. These locations and landmarks would have been recognizable, even precious, to the first generations of Israelites living in Canaan, but these words and descriptions are meaningless to most readers today.

Still, no Christian should denigrate any portion of Holy Scripture. We believe correctly that all Scripture is given by the inspiration of God and is profitable (2 Timothy 3:16–17). This commitment must include even lengthy geographically specific descriptions. It is easy to see why these details might be in a property deed, but why are they forever in the Bible? How are they profitable? For at least two practical reasons and one spiritual.

First, these detailed allotments hindered conflict. By recording the specific boundaries and resource apportionment of each tribe, Joshua and the priests performed an end run around future intra-national disputes. The authority of the Lord himself was understood and appealed to throughout the process. Questioning the allotments would be questioning the Lord. Eventually, the tribes would still fight over land, but clearly defining the territories at the outset lessened this going forward.

Second, these detailed allotments established the potential of Israel's inheritance. With the detailed layout, each tribe could see the territory they were to subdue and grow into. Occupying the whole allotted land would take diligent effort through multiple generations. Failure to occupy it would lead to trouble through multiple generations. This helps to explain the ongoing warfare we read about in the later historical books and the religious and cultural threats Israel endured from the surrounding people groups they did not subdue. By laying out the potential, Joshua provided a specific measure for assessing success or failure in following the Lord's command to conquer.

Third, these detailed allotments of the territories support Joshua's historicity. Critics of the Bible often suggest that its accounts are mythological or etiological.[20] However, a large portion of the Bible is dedicated to genealogy, materials lists, building specs, and geographic descriptions. Mythology, grounded in religious ideals rather than reality, seldom mentions such minutiae. History, on the other hand, has an interest in accurately chronicling what happened. For religions as bound to historical events as Judaism and Christianity, historicity is indispensable. Joshua's allotment details indicate that the Joshua conquest was an actual historical event and should bolster our confidence in the Bible.

So we study the allotment passages of Joshua to give us historical understanding and assurance in the reliability of God's Word. Along the way, we will also turn off at some points of interest that pique our curiosity.

Land Still Unclaimed

To this point, the conquest of Canaan was a breathtaking success. Every king who conspired to wipe out Israel was wiped out. Every city that resisted takeover was taken over. All the armies were disarmed. It reads quickly, but it took a long time (Joshua 11:18). There was yet more fighting to do, still more territory to claim.

- *What natural limitation motivated Joshua and the Lord to allocate the land (Joshua 13:1)? What are some obvious implications of Joshua's age? How old do you estimate he was?*

- *What specific unsubdued people group in the southwest would prove to be a giant problem to Israel (vv. 2–3)? What does the Lord promise to do about the Sidonians in the north (v. 6)?*

- *How did God want Joshua to think about the still unconquered regions (vv. 6–7)?*

As we learned on Joshua's inauguration day, some of the Israelites already had their allotted lands. The tribes of Gad, Reuben, and half of the tribe of Manasseh conquered and claimed land on the east side of the Jordan. The families of these tribes were already settled in the cities conquered there, and their livestock were already feeding in the pasture lands.

Moses had already apportioned these Transjordan lands (Numbers 32:33–42; Deuteronomy 3:8–17), so Joshua reviewed the boundaries of those territories (Joshua 13:8–13, 15–32), before moving on to the others in Canaan. The rest of the apportioning occurred in two stages—the two most powerful tribes and then the rest.

Borders Begin

- *What personalities were involved in the parceling of the land in Canaan (Joshua 14:1, 5)? Why would these have taken part in this important and permanent process? What is the significance of each person listed?*

- *What tribes are mentioned as special cases (vv. 3–4)?*

The Lion's Share

- *What tribe was the first to come for their inheritance (v. 6)? What member of that tribe was the first to receive his? Who was his only peer in Israel?*

- *What story did Caleb retell before he demanded his allocation (vv. 6–9)? What promise did God make to him decades before?*

- *How old was Caleb when the allotments began (vv. 10–11)? How was his health holding up in his old age? Was he looking forward to retirement?*

- *What life goals did he still have in mind (v. 12)? What group of people was he decidedly not afraid of? How could he possibly accomplish his courageous goals?*

• *How did Joshua respond to the confidence of Caleb (vv. 13–15)?*

• *Was Caleb successful in his endeavors (15:13–19)? Support your answer.*

• *What adjectives would you use to describe Caleb?*

The first time Israel came to the promised land, only Caleb and Joshua believed that the Lord could keep his promises. The other spies had the same facts but came to a different conclusion: there was no way Israel could win a campaign against the people who lived there. Caleb didn't believe that. He knew then that God was powerful enough to conquer all their enemies. He still believed it four decades later.

As a result of Israel's unbelief, the Lord condemned all of them over twenty years old to die in the wilderness. Since they would not go into the land by the command and power of God, they would not go in at all. As a result, Caleb was the oldest living Israelite.

How much would we expect from an octogenarian today? Would we scour the nursing homes or country clubs for a leader to go into battle? Age played no part in Caleb's decision except as an additional reason to boast in the sustaining power of God to do amazing things. Wasn't the Lord good to allow this faithful, fearless, wholehearted follower the first portion of land?

Caleb is the standout, but the rest of the tribe of Judah received their inheritance that day too (15:1–12, 20–63). Generations before, Jacob gave his fourth son, Judah, the blessing of the first-born (Genesis 49:8–12), and it is obvious in the apportionment. They received the largest portion of land by far—land that had the greatest number of developed cities. Israel's greatest kings would come from this tribe, including the Messiah, the Lion of the tribe of Judah (Revelation 5:4–5).

 THE BACKSTORY

Joseph was Jacob's favorite son. His story of the coat of many colors and the fraternal strife that came from his father's special treatment is a saga of its own (Genesis 37, 39–50). God used the family discord for good (50:19–21), though, and rescued the whole family. The history of Israel as a people delivered from bondage starts there.

While in Egypt, restored to his long-lost son, Jacob claimed both of Joseph's boys as his own children (48:3–6). So rather than Joseph becoming a single tribe like the rest of his brothers, Ephraim and Manasseh became the heads of two separate tribes (Joshua 14:4). This is apparent in the allotments of Joshua 16–17.

First, Ephraim's descendants were granted their lands (Joshua 16) and then the other half of Manasseh's tribe received theirs (Joshua 17).

- *What special case was settled for the descendants of Manasseh (17:3–6)? This was an extraordinary concession for that cultural era. The Bible is sometimes accused of misogyny. How does this passage speak to that issue?*

- *What complaint did the people of Manasseh bring against Joshua's allotments (v. 14)? Did Joshua agree with their objection (v. 15)?*

- *What solution did Joshua offer? What did they think of his suggestion (v. 16)?*

- *Compare this to Caleb's attitude in 14:12. How did their character differ?*

- *Did Joshua back down (17:17–18)? What did he demand they do with their extra parcel?*

The attitude of this tribe was almost completely opposite that of Caleb. Instead of seizing the opportunity that God offered them, they demanded more land and an easier assignment. In fact, they sounded more like their forefathers, who refused to take the land in the first place. They could only see their enemies' strength and war machinery and not the faithfulness of God. Joshua saw through their complaint, insisting that faith and hard work would get the job done.

Rest for the Rest

After Joshua had made these assignments, time passed, and the Israelite camp moved from Gilgal to Shiloh, where the people set up the Tabernacle. This new site became the location of worship for hundreds of years until the days of Samuel. Here, Joshua made the final allotments (18:1–2).

- *Why does Joshua seem frustrated with the remaining tribes (18:3)?*

- *What plan did Joshua make to parcel out the remaining territory (vv. 4–10)? How many surveyors did he tell the people to appoint? How many territories did they divide out?*

- *Who would determine which tribes received which allotments? How would they decide this?*

Joshua took much care to ensure impartiality. He had the people choose the surveyors from every remaining tribe. This team unambiguously defined the seven divisions. They wrote down the descriptions on a scroll so that there would be no hearsay or misunderstanding. Finally, to avoid any partiality or the appearance of it, Joshua assigned these territories to each tribe by casting lots. No one understood this as a chance decision though. This was the process that the Lord used to clearly make his will known to them all (vv. 1, 6, 8, 10)

One by one, Joshua assigned each section of land, casting lots to determine which tribe would receive that section. So the tribes of Benjamin (18:11–28), Simeon (19:1–9), Zebulun (19:10–16), Issachar (vv. 17–23), Asher (vv. 24–31), Naphtali (vv. 32–39), and Dan (vv. 40–48) received their inheritances through this process.

- *What was unusual about the territory Joshua assigned to the tribe of Simeon (19:9)?*

- *What happened when Dan's tribe attempted to secure the land they were assigned (v. 47)?*

At last, all the land was divided among the tribes. Their boundaries marked each inheritance, and the assignments were clear. Whatever territory remained to be developed would be up to the tribe assigned to that land. Whatever enemies still lived in the region, the tribe assigned to that land needed to deal with them. Diligence, effort, and faithfulness would ensure success.[21]

🌀 DIGGING DEEPER

The family gathers around the attorney's desk. Well-dressed and stocked with tissues, they have recently lost their beloved relative. Now they have gathered for the reading of the will. One-by-one, the attorney reads their names aloud and the new possessions their loved one has granted. There is no negotiating and no changing the terms. Whether they are elated or disappointed, at the end of this process, their inheritance is settled.

An inheritance comes to us not by our own effort but as a gift. It is not something anyone owes to us but a gracious choice based on our relationship with our departed relative. Inheritance is meant to be a blessing to the heir.

For Israel, the land was a long-promised inheritance. More than two hundred times, the Old Testament designates it that way. It was the gracious choice of the Lord to select Abraham out of all the people in the world. It was God's grace to promise Abraham's descendants a place in the world. It was his grace that rescued them from slavery, led them to Canaan, and conquered their enemies. He gave the land to them because he loved them. No other reason. It was not Israel's size or strength or character that got them this fertile land. It was all a gracious gift.

Believers today understand this too. God does not owe us a single blessing. Our rebel hearts have disqualified us from ever making that demand. But the Lord, in his great mercy, has given us "every spiritual blessing in the heavenly realm" (Ephesians 1:3). It is a gracious gift. Nothing more (2:8–9).

- *Read the following passages about our inheritance as followers of Jesus. What specific blessings do we inherit? Jot a prayer of thankfulness to God for that gracious gift to you.*

	Thank you, Lord, for the gracious gift of…
Matthew 5:3–5	
Matthew 19:27–30	
Romans 8:16–21	
Ephesians 1:13–21	
Colossians 1:9–14	
Titus 3:4–7	
Hebrews 6:11–12	
1 Peter 1:3–5	
Revelation 21:1–7	

What an incredible inheritance you have given me in
Christ! Amen.

One Last Portion

The apportionments began with the oldest man in Israel, one of the two faithful spies. The process ended with territory for the other. Finally, after decades of wandering, camping, scouting, praying, leading, fighting, and toiling, Joshua could have his own place to call home.

- *Who gave Joshua his portion of the land (Joshua 19:49–50)? Who commanded them to give it?*

- *His tribe, Ephraim, had already been assigned land (Joshua 16). Where was Joshua's portion? Who chose the parcel for him? Was it move-in ready?*

- *The allotment process ends with a review. What personalities oversaw the entire process (19:51)? How do we know that this process had the Lord's direction and approval?*

EXPERIENCE GOD'S HEART

- *What portions of the Bible are you tempted to skim over or skip entirely? Does it help to see that detailed lists of places and names demonstrate the Bible's reliability?*

- *If there were such a thing as a Holy Devotion Gauge, Caleb's would have been pinned at 100 percent. Where would you place the Holy Devotion Gauge reading for the tribe of Joseph? What about your own church? What about your own heart?*

❤ SHARE GOD'S HEART

- *The young people in your life are casting about for an example. Many of them will find it in a celebrity or activist. What if there were an imitation-worthy, godly example in their lives? What about you? Is there someone you could take under your wing and show them Caleb-like spiritual courage?*

- *Begin praying for this person today, including asking God to open up opportunities for you to begin setting a courageous and godly example for this individual to follow.*

Talking It Out

1. Old Caleb seemed in no mood to retire. What are your thoughts about the courage and faith of senior saints? Is there an appropriate time to step back from tackling great endeavors? Is there a right age or stage to retire from Christian ministries?

2. Read about each of the spiritual inheritances from the previous Digging Deeper section. Discuss which ones stand out for each participant. Explain why that is so.

LESSON 10

Safe Spaces

(Joshua 20–21)

For many 1960s TV fans, Dr. Richard Kimble was a familiar face best known as *The Fugitive*. He was falsely accused and convicted for the murder of his own wife and sentenced to death. Then he escaped when his prison train derailed. Each episode he sought the true killer while simultaneously being hunted by the unyielding police detective, Lieutenant Philip Gerard.

Gerard did not concern himself with whether Kimble was actually a murderer. He was only interested in enforcing the law. In his view, a man whom the courts had determined to be guilty, rightly or wrongly, must be punished. So Kimble ran and ran and ran from him...for one hundred twenty episodes. What this innocent man needed was a refuge from the enforcer.

The Fugitive was fiction, but innocent fugitives were a reality in ancient Israel. Now that each tribe had a place to be, their fugitives needed a place to run. The Lord had a plan.

Sanctuary!

- *Who was responsible for providing a place for innocent fugitives (Joshua 20:1–3)? What sort of person would be allowed to flee there? Whom were they fleeing from?*

- *What authorities would an innocent fugitive seek out when they came to a city of refuge (v. 4)? What were their responsibilities to the fugitive (vv. 4–5)?*

- *How long could the fugitive receive shelter in the city of refuge (v. 6)? What two things could end their refuge in that city? When would they be free to return home?*

Ancient Israel had no courts or lawyers, no jails or probation officers. However, they did have a justice system. When a case was brought before them, local elders or priests would evaluate cases and accusations. They would weigh the evidence and consult the law of Moses. Then they would pronounce judgment. Most sentences were spelled out in the law.

The legal consequence for murder was death. There was no death row in ancient Israel, no lethal injection. Instead, a close relative of the victim was designated to be the avenger of blood. This individual was then duty bound to carry out a death sentence against the murderer. Any person credibly accused of murder was liable to be killed by the avenger of blood.

However, accidents happen. Not every killing was murder. Sometimes a death was accidental, and when it was, there needed to be some other merciful solution, especially in the case where there was bad blood between the families to begin with. The cities of refuge, like the medieval Christian sanctuary, provided a safe space from the enforcer.[22] They were placed within walking or running distance for every tribe in Israel.

As the chief judicial figure in Israel, the high priest's authority over the innocent fugitive was acknowledged. By demanding sanctuary, the fugitive became a *de facto* servant of the high priest. Confined to stay within the boundaries of the city of refuge, the fugitive's old life was over, and he required a new vocation. Since every refuge city was also a city of Levites (Joshua 21), there would have been many roles available for assisting the priests. The innocent fugitive would remain a ward of the high priest until the high priest's death.

 # DIGGING DEEPER

The high priest had the most important human role in Israel. His ongoing duties kept the nation oriented around the Lord. He offered atoning sacrifices for sin. He led the community in public worship. He represented God to the people and the people before God. He instructed the nation in the righteous ways of the law.

Every Israelite needed the high priest to perform these religious tasks, but for the innocent fugitive, the high priest was his lifeline. It was his official role and authority that sheltered the fugitive from death when he fled to his refuge. Having come under his salvation from death, the fugitive owed his allegiance and service to the high priest. Furthermore, only the death of the high priest himself could restore freedom to the fugitive.

The reflective Christian will have no trouble seeing obvious parallels with Jesus. The writer of Hebrews in the New Testament was transfixed by the similarities. In his letter he mentions the high priestly role eighteen times, almost all of them as a meditation on Christ's ministry to us in salvation and new life in him.

But the writer of Hebrews wasn't only explaining how Jesus was *like* the high priest in Israel; he wanted his readers to understand why Jesus is *better*.

- *Read the following passages from Hebrews and see if you can discover how Jesus is like and better than the high priest in Israel.*

How Jesus is like Israel's high priest		How Jesus is a better high priest
	Hebrews 2:14–18	
	Hebrews 4:14–16	
	Hebrews 5:1–10	

	Hebrews 6:16–20	
	Hebrews 7:23–28	
	Hebrews 8:1–6	
	Hebrews 9:6–15	

Israel's Parsonage Towns

In 1820, Reverend Patrick relocated his wife and four young children to northern England where he began a long tenure as minister with St. Michael's and All Angels Church of England. The family lived quite comfortably there in the church parsonage for many years. During the terminal illness of Patrick's young wife, his sister-in-law joined the family to tend the children, and a Yorkshire maid entertained the family with local stories as she cooked. The Haworth parish house, provided by the church for their minister's family, was fertile ground for the imagination. While living there, this curate's remarkable children penned *Jane Eyre*, *Wuthering Heights*, *Agnes Grey*, *The Tenant of Wildfell Hall*, *Emma,* and dozens of noteworthy poems. Admirers of the Brontë family who visit the Brontë Parsonage Museum can still tour the parsonage today.

Parsonages, sometimes called manses, vicarages, parish houses, or rectories, were once a standard feature of church property. To ensure that the church minister's housing needs were provided, a comfortable home was built near the church, often on the same property. When touring England, it is unusual to find a stone church that does not have such a house. Churches felt an obligation to secure housing for their religious leaders, so the manse was included in the minister's compensation. It was only right.

The careful reader of the tribal allocations in Joshua 13–19 will notice one tribe still homeless at the end of the lot casting at Shiloh. This tribe played a key role in Israel, that of religious leadership. Some of them were the priests. All of them tended to the tabernacle and its furnishings (Numbers 1:50–53; 3:5–10).

They had been active participants in the conquest. In fact, no Israelite would have crossed the Jordan River without them stepping into the water. And Jericho would have remained standing if these religious leaders had not led the march around the town. Even in the land divisions for all the others, one member of their tribe was present to oversee the process and ensure the approval of God.

The Levites needed homes. It was only right for the community to look after their religious leaders' housing. The Lord had a plan.

• *After all the land distribution for each tribe was completed, the Levites came with their appeal. What two specific assets did they ask for (Joshua 21:1–2)? On whose authority did they ask?*

- *Where did the property for the Levites come from (vv. 3, 41–42)?*

- *What tabernacle responsibilities were the Kohathites assigned (Numbers 3:31–32, 38)? The Gershonites (vv. 25–26)? The Merarites (vv. 36–37)? These three clans of Levites received their cities by lot just like the other tribes (Joshua 21:4–8).*

THE BACKSTORY

As Moses allotted the land to the tribes, he reiterated one point throughout: the Levites needed no inheritance; they had the Lord. "Moses gave no inheritance of land to the tribe of Levi, but said to them, 'Yahweh, the God of Israel, is to be your inheritance'" (Joshua 13:33).

God's special relationship with the Levites began in Moses' time. Moses and his brother Aaron were great-grandsons of Levi (Exodus 6:16–20). They led the Israelites for four decades. But the event that really set the Levites apart from the rest of the tribes was the embarrassing incident of the golden calf (Exodus 32).

When Moses came down the mountain to find Israel worshiping this ridiculous statue and degrading themselves in front of it, he asked a question, "Who is on the LORD's side?" With all the infidelity going on, would anyone be faithful to God (v. 26 ESV)? One tribe answered his challenge: the Levites. They came to Moses, strapped on their swords, and wreaked judgment on the people for their outrageous sin against God. In the middle of all that chaos, Moses made this pronouncement: "Today you have been ordained for the service of the LORD, each one at the cost of his son and of his brother, so that he might bestow a blessing upon you this day" (v. 29 ESV).

Later, God coupled the Levites with his principle of *redemption*. The last and greatest plague in Egypt, the one that finally buckled the Pharaoh, was the death of Egypt's firstborn children. The night of the plague, God sent his destroying angel through the land, striking down any firstborn. This would have happened to the Israelites, too, except that God provided protection. Any family that killed a lamb and daubed its blood on their doorposts would be passed over. Here are the roots of the Passover festival (12:21–30).

As a result, the Lord declared that every firstborn belonged to him. He spared them when they otherwise would have been killed. To acknowledge this, every firstborn had to be redeemed, purchased back from the Lord, with a sacrifice (13:11–13). This practice lasted until God substituted the entire Levite tribe for the firstborn sons of Israel (Numbers 3:11–13, 40–41) in the first thorough census of Israel. From then on, every Levite belonged to God as the price for Israel's redemption.

Along with this special relationship, the Lord gave the Levites special responsibilities and privileges. They were allowed to be closer to his holy presence than any others. Theirs was the priesthood, including the high priesthood. They offered the sacrifices. They could handle the ark of the covenant. They ministered in the tabernacle and tended its furnishings. These privileges granted them the honor and respect of the rest of the Israelites.

In all these promises of an intangible inheritance, God also made provision for their practical needs. They were allowed to eat from the offerings the rest of their countrymen made at the altar (Numbers 18:8–10; Deuteronomy 18:1–5). The Israelites were to give a tithe, a tenth, of their wealth toward providing for the Levites (Numbers 18:20–24; Deuteronomy 14:22–29). Finally, the Israelites would provide the Levites with towns to live in and the pasture-lands around those towns for their livestock (Numbers 35:2–5).

That is why the Levites were not granted any property by the usual allocation. Their ministry was to the Lord and all the people, so the Lord and all the people provided for them. It was only right.

Promised Land

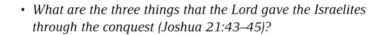

- *What are the three things that the Lord gave the Israelites through the conquest (Joshua 21:43–45)?*

- *What was Israel's role in securing each of these gifts?*

- *How many times are the promises of God mentioned in these verses? How complete was his promise-keeping? Hint: Look for words like "all" and "every."*

These three understated verses are the conclusion of a journey that lasted hundreds of years. From the day that God spoke to Abraham in Ur (Genesis 12:1–3), telling him to leave his father's household, this people group has been on the move. Abraham, Isaac, and Jacob always lived in tents.

Joseph got to live in a palace but only after some time in a pit, in slavery, and in prison. Egypt never felt like home to him. Even after he ruled there and moved his family to Egypt to survive the brutal famine, Joseph made his children promise that they would bury his bones in Canaan.

Before long, Joseph's descendants were not the welcome guests of Egypt but slaves subjected to harsh labor. For generations of slavery, the Israelites longed for release and home. Through Moses, they finally got free from bondage and through the sea only to languish for forty years in the wilderness.

Then came the conquest with more years of tenting, fighting, scouting, and surveying. Now, after all that homelessness, every Israelite had a home. From the oldest to the newest, the least to the greatest, they had a place to belong. Because God kept his promises. Every promise. Not one of his promises failed.

The Lord had a plan.

⬥ EXPERIENCE GOD'S HEART

- *Have you ever been wrongly accused? What were the consequences of that? What effect did that innocent suffering have on your view of the Lord?*

- *What does it mean to you that God provided places for the falsely accused to run for refuge?*

- *As God Incarnate, Jesus represented the Lord to us. As a divine human being, he could represent us to the Lord. Jesus offered the atoning sacrifice for our sins once for all. Isn't that the best news you ever heard! Pray through the ways that Jesus is a better high priest for you.*

 # SHARE GOD'S HEART

While the Lord had a plan to provide for faithful ministers, all of us know someone who was harmed by an unfaithful representative of God. Sadly, physical, emotional, sexual, or religious abuse is shockingly common in the church. Sometimes these experiences drive people away from any level of faith at all.

We can help people who have suffered these injuries. We can pray for them about it, of course. We can be a nonjudgmental listening ear for them. We can help them distinguish between the Lord and people who claim to represent him. In our character and behavior, we can represent the Lord to them, showing them that some of God's people are safe.

Talking It Out

1. Paul taught his readers that "pastors who lead the church well should be paid well. They should receive double honor for faithfully preaching and teaching the revelation of the Word of God" (1 Timothy 5:17). How is this principle similar to God's provision for the Levites? How is it different? What is your viewpoint toward providing financially for Christian leaders?

2. After traveling a long and winding road, Israel was finally home. Many of us have had a circuitous journey to find a spiritual home. Describe yours to the others. How did you come to the church where you worship? Can you call it your spiritual home?

LESSON 11

Together in Truth and Love

(Joshua 22)

Trolling. Flaming. Ghosting.

In our day, instant condemnation of others is too easy. An online troll does not have to know the person they criticize. They do not even have to know much about the person they criticize. They simply sit down at the computer, think up a half-witty retort, and let it fly. This is sport to some. No matter the fallout for others, it's good fun. And if things get intense or difficult for the troll, they drop out of the interaction. They don't reply. They don't reconcile. They just disappear.

This is uncivil behavior for anyone, of course, but when Christians troll or flame one another, it is appalling. For the people of Jesus, the Prince of Peace, to revel in dissension is a disgrace. Still, this treatment is everywhere. Search the internet for any Christian author or teacher that you admire. Dozens of articles, postings, even whole websites will appear, dedicated to knocking them down.

A well-known Christian author wrote a book in which he singled out a Colorado pastor as a false prophet. A ministry friend asked the pastor, "Did that author ever phone you? Did you ever talk about these issues?" There was heartache in the pastor's answer. "No, the first time I learned that he had a problem with my teaching was in his book." The author had aired their doctrinal differences in a nationally publicized and marketed book. Shameful.

When Christians flame authors and teachers online or in print without even giving them a chance to explain themselves, we need a reset. When others inside the body of Christ at one time or another call every well-known Christian teacher a heretic or a compromiser, we need to repent. With so many divisions in the church of Christ, we could learn from the Israelites. A lesson fresh from the completed conquest, the lesson of truth and love.

Mission Accomplished

- *How did Joshua summarize the follow-through of the Transjordan tribes (Joshua 22:1–3)? Who had they obeyed over the long years of conquest?*

- *As Joshua released these faithful warriors to return to their families and properties, what exhortation did he give them (v. 5)? List the five commands he gave them in this single verse. What measure of devotion were they to give toward this?*

- *What did Joshua do for them as they left (vv. 6–7)? What evidence did they take with them proving it had been a successful conquest?*

Joshua called the Reubenites, Gadites, and half of the Manassehites together. He told them, *You guys did it. You did it. You kept your word. You followed Moses, and you followed me. Now go back to your homes and to your families, but don't forget to love the Lord wholeheartedly.*

In Lesson 2, we learned that Moses already gave these tribes their own territory on the east side of the Jordan. When Israel crossed over the Jordan to begin the conquest of Canaan, the soldiers from these tribes were obliged to lead the charge. It was only fair. Since the other tribes fought King Og and King Sihon to secure property for the tribes of Reuben, Gad, and half of the Manasseh, they fought faithfully for the rest of Israel.

They kept their promises. They went into the land ahead of the Israelites. This was some commitment. Israel was longer in their conquest than any country that fought in World War I or World War II. Reuben, Gad, and half of the Manasseh spent seven years without their families, whom they left behind on the other side of the river. They fought day after day to help the other ten tribes secure a homeland. Now, along with the rest of the soldiers, the Reubenites, the Gadites, and the Manassehites were war-weary and relieved to go home.

Fighting for Truth

- *When the two-and-a-half tribes came back to the crossing point, what religious building project did they complete (v. 10)?*

- *How did the rest of the tribes feel about this altar (vv. 11–12)? Why do you think the altar was a problem?*

- *What were the ten tribes prepared to do about this?*

Just as they crossed the river back into their territory, they stopped to build an enormous altar that could be seen from a long way off. Through Moses, God commanded Israel to build the tabernacle (Exodus 27). The tabernacle was the place where the people kept the ark of the covenant, where they preserved the book of the law, where the priests ministered before the Lord in worship and offerings, and where Israel was always supposed to offer their worship. More importantly, it was the one place that God filled with his glory (40:34–38).

The tabernacle with its altar was located at Shiloh (Joshua 18:1), where it would rest for three-and-a-half centuries. This place was already the religious capital of Israel. But now, as these tribes departed for their own land east of the Jordan, they built this new, imposing altar. In that move, the spiritual unity of God's holy people was at stake.

To demonstrate what a serious breach of fellowship this was, the rest of the country gathered to go to war against the Reubenites, the Gadites, and the Manassehites. After more than seven years of fighting, they were willing to return to war, a religious civil war, to protect their nation against idolatry. They were unblinkingly zealous for faithfulness to God alone. Even if these were their brothers, they were their enemies if they made an enemy of God. There were some truths worth fighting and dying for. The preeminence of the one true God was certainly one of those truths.

Israel was willing to fight for the truth. That was amazing progress! When they first came out of Egypt and witnessed the Lord's benevolent power as they crossed the Red Sea, they went to Mount Sinai to meet with him. But before Moses even came down with the first part of the Law, they were worshiping the golden calf at the base of the mountain. While the one true God was speaking to Moses, they were worshiping an idol.

THE BACKSTORY

In their wanderings through the desert, they dabbled in idolatry again. In Numbers 22–25 we read that King Balak of Moab saw what happened to King Og and King Sihon. In fear, he decided the best course of action was to put a curse on Israel. So he called the local prophet Balaam to come and pronounce a curse against them, but try as he might, Balaam couldn't curse them. Every time he opened his mouth, blessing after blessing would pour out (24:10–11). It was no use. God would not allow Balaam to succeed.

When King Balak finally gave up, Prophet Balaam had an idea. He proposed another strategy. Balaam taught Balak that the Moabite women could seduce the men of Israel. The women could engage in sexual immorality with the Israelite men and draw them into the pagan worship of Baal, the fertility god (see 25:1–3; 31:16; Revelation 2:14). They tried it at a place called Peor. This strategy worked, and Israel plummeted into idolatry almost overnight. In fact, a man named Zimri was so brazen about his idolatry and his adultery that he paraded his pagan lover right through the camp and into his tent (Numbers 25:6–9). That's when Phineas, the son of the high priest, ran out of patience. He took his spear into Zimri's tent and impaled them both. Phineas was so zealous for God's honor that day that God chose him to be the future high priest (vv. 10–13).

Now in Joshua's day, potential idolatry brought Israel to the brink of war. This nation, so prone to idolatry in the past, was ready to fight their own brothers over the truth when they saw the enormous altar the two-and-a-half tribes had built. The whole nation gathered at the Holy Place, Shiloh, for battle.

However, their willingness to fight for truth was matched by their commitment to love. Before they went to war, they confronted their brothers in love.

Confronting in Love

• *Whom did Israel send in the delegation to confront the two-and-a-half tribes (Joshua 22:13–14)? Why was it significant that Phineas was there?*

• *Why did every other tribe send a representative?*

• *What four things did the delegation accuse them of doing with this altar (vv. 15–18)? Whose accusations are these (v. 16)?*

• *What two recent incidents did the delegation raise as examples of God's judgment against Israel (vv. 17, 20)? What were the divine consequences on the whole community for those sins?*

• *What is the nub of their contention against the Transjordan tribes' altar (v. 19)?*

From the Peor incident, we know that Phineas was a fanatic for God's honor. Knowing that he led this delegation shows how serious they were in addressing this conflict. When they caught up with the Transjordan tribes, they did not mince words. They accused them of terrible things: breaking faith, rebellion, turning away, unfaithfulness. They compared the new altar to the idolatry and treachery of Peor. They compared them to Achan, the thief, who brought calamity on them all at Ai. Everyone would suffer if some of them abandoned the Lord. These were hard words.

Surprise Agreement

- *When the Transjordan tribes answered, they agreed with the convictions of the others. How do we know this from their answer (vv. 22–23)?*

- *Clearly, the ten tribes misunderstood their gesture, but who understood them perfectly? Who knew their true intent (v. 22)?*

- *Did they build that great altar as a rival altar to worship at the tabernacle (v. 23)? What concern motivated them to build the new altar (vv. 24–25)?*

- *What was the reasoning behind erecting the altar at the Jordan River crossing (vv. 26–28)? What role did they want the altar to play among the tribes (vv. 27–28)? How can an inanimate object be a witness?*

- *What did the Transjordan tribes publicly commit themselves to do together with the other tribes (v. 29)? Where was worship in Israel to take place?*

The Transjordan tribes explained themselves. They agreed with everything their brothers were saying. An altar for worship to rival the altar at Shiloh would be a heinous sin. Erecting an altar to distract their tribes from God's presence and instruction at the tabernacle would be spiritually dangerous. If these accusations were correct, the Transjordan tribes had done a tremendous evil and deserved punishment.

But there wasn't evil; there was misunderstanding. In fact, the Transjordan tribes' chief concern was that, in the future, they would be separated from the rest of Israel by more than a river. They were concerned that there would come a day when the rest of the nation would write them off and exclude them from the worship of the one true God. So they built an altar, a giant pile of stones, to remind those on the east *and* those on the west that the tribes on both sides of the Jordan belonged to Israel and that they always would.

The Resolution of Truth and Love

· *Was the answer given by the Transjordan tribes
satisfactory to Phineas and the delegation (v. 30)? What
did their answer prove to the delegation (v. 31)? Because
of their true motives, what was Israel spared?*

· *The delegation returned to Shiloh to report the results of
their confrontation. How did the rest of Israel feel about
the conclusions (vv. 32–33)?*

· *What did they name the new altar (v. 34)? What truths
did it represent?*

This explanation satisfied even Phineas, zealot for the Lord and fanatic for God's honor and glory. The tribes cleared up the misunderstanding, they restored peace, and they gave this new altar the name Witness. That altar would stand there as a witness for centuries, a witness between them that both peoples acknowledged the same God.

We can imagine how this story would have turned out differently without a willingness to fight for truth. The other tribes would have shrugged when another altar was raised on their border. They might have concluded, "What's the big deal? It's just a pile of rocks. Maybe they're using it to worship the true God, maybe not. Certainly, it's no hill to die on. Let's just love our brothers and get on with the settling of the land." Harmony would have trumped holiness, and compromise would have been easy.

However, by taking such a strong stand against even potential idolatry, the leaders made it clear that they would brook no false worship. They would oppose any abandonment of the Lord. "Israel was faithful to serve Yahweh during the lifetime of Joshua and the lifetime of the elders who lived on after Joshua, those who had experienced all the miracles that Yahweh had done for Israel" (24:31).

Because they took a firm stand that day and were willing to fight for truth, even against their brothers, they protected an entire generation from swerving away from the Lord. There had never been a generation without idolatry, but this generation was faithful to God, and their passionate devotion to the truth guaranteed it.

We can also imagine this episode without love. Israel would have strapped on their swords and launched a war grounded in a misunderstanding, resulting in untold casualties in a permanently divided nation. They would have charged across the river, killing their brothers and devastating their land. Fanaticism would have trumped family and splintered the people of God forever.

Because they confronted in love, because they went to talk it through before they went to war, that whole disaster was averted. Obviously, they doubted the motives of the altar builders, but before they went to war based on those suspicions, they listened to the explanation of the other side.

What they discovered is that the others had identical convictions. What a tragedy it would have been if they had gone to war, taking up arms against people with identical convictions! Instead, through loving confrontation, they found people agreeing that there must be no rival worship. So they didn't fight because they didn't need to. Truth wasn't compromised after all, and love clarified that.

 DIGGING DEEPER

Conflict and confrontation are a fact of life, even for Christians. Sometimes it is over petty things. Sometimes it is over misunderstandings like Israel experienced that day. Sometimes it is disagreement about strategy. Sometimes it is sin that needs correction. In serious disagreement, we are still urged toward unity.

> I urge you, my brothers and sisters, for the sake of the name of our Lord Jesus Christ, to agree to live in unity with one another and put to rest any division that attempts to tear you apart. Be restored as one united body living in perfect harmony. Form a consistent choreography among yourselves, having a common perspective with shared values. (1 Corinthians 1:10)

- *The Bible gives Christians thorough directions for maintaining unity by managing differences with other believers with grace. Read the following Scripture passages and answer these questions:*

    › *Is the problem a sin or heresy, a misunderstanding, or a strategy?*

› *What is the role of truth and love in dealing with each instance?*

Passage	Problem	Role of Truth	Role of Love
Matthew 18:15–20			
Acts 15:36–41			
1 Corinthians 5:1–6			
Galatians 6:1–5			
Ephesians 4:14–15			
Colossians 3:12–14			
1 Thessalonians 3:6–15			

Unity in the family of God depends on love *and* truth. There is no unity where there is no truth. We cannot be likeminded when we don't agree on the basic tenets of faith. Where truth does not matter, there can be no unity.

And there cannot be unity where there is no love. Unity without love is not the truth anyway. Followers of the one true God must love the truth *and* be true to love. It is the only way that the people of God can remain unified in him.

 EXPERIENCE GOD'S HEART

- *Most Christians lean one way or another. Some are activists about truth. Some are fanatics about love. Which way do you lean? Do you think it is possible to be balanced regarding these two principles of healthy fellowship? Why or why not?*

- *When either truth or love is prioritized over the other, friendships can fray. Have you lost a friendship over this? Did you flame someone or ghost them? Did they do that to you? What truth and love steps can you take to reconcile this relationship?*

❤ SHARE GOD'S HEART

- *Presenting the gospel implies a confrontation. The truth of the gospel will challenge the status quo in an individual's beliefs or self-perception. Can the gospel be presented without love? What if we "love" someone so much that we avoid confronting them with the truth? Is that what we should do? Why or why not?*

Talking It Out

1. Do you know anyone like Phineas? Are you a "Phineas"? Talk about why having someone like him, a zealot for truth and God's honor, is necessary in the church. What trouble can a Phineas create for fellowship? How does a mature Phineas demonstrate love?

2. Which principle, truth or love, do you think the contemporary church most emphasizes? What problems is this causing inside the church? What conflicts is it causing between the church and surrounding society? Is there a culturally acceptable solution?

LESSON 12

Decision Point

(Joshua 23–24)

"'How long will you waver between two opinions? If the LORD is God, follow him; but if Baal is God, follow him.' But the people said nothing" (1 Kings 18:21 NIV). Their non-choice began a day-long duel between the prophet of the one true God and eight hundred and fifty priests of the Canaanite deity Baal (vv. 21–39).

The pagan priests took the first turn in the competition. They spent the long day chanting and moaning, circling and shouting, leaping and slashing themselves, creating a reeking, slimy mud track around their altar to the chief god of the Amorites. All the while, there was deafening silence from Baal. He didn't answer because he couldn't answer. And yet Israel and these pagan prophets had chosen to worship Baal.

Then Elijah stepped up, called the people to him, and prepared his altar.

The contrast was stark. Baal's altar to one side, abandoned by the people. Baal's bull carcass, abuzz with flies and putrefying in the sun, with panting, bloody priests collapsed all around it. Elijah's altar neatly arranged, freshly rebuilt, dripping with clear water, and surrounded by the people. This altar was attended by a single confident prophet of God.

Elijah prayed a simple prayer, "LORD, the God of Abraham, Isaac and Israel, let it be known today that you are God in Israel and that I am your servant and have done all these things at your command. Answer me, LORD, answer me, so these people will know that you, LORD, are God, and that you are turning their hearts back again" (vv. 36–37 NIV).

Then the fire of the Lord fell and burned up the sacrifice, the wood, the stones, the dirt, and licked up the water in the trench. When the people saw this, they fell prostrate and cried, "The LORD—he is God! The LORD—he is God!" (v. 39).

Five hundred years earlier and forty-five miles away, another leader had called the same people to make the same choice. Which would they serve, the gods of the Canaanites or the one true God?

Joshua's Final Farewell

- *Whom specifically did Joshua call to meet with him as he began his farewells (Joshua 23:1–2)? Was Israel still fighting the conquest at this point?*

- *Whom did Joshua credit with the success of the conquest (vv. 3–4)? How could both parties receive the credit?*

• *What work was left to be done (v. 5)? Who would do it?*

• *Joshua gave two familiar commands to these leaders. Compare 23:6 to 1:7. Why was this instruction that was originally given to Joshua repeated by him to these leaders at this stage in their history?*

• *What danger could steer them away from faithfulness to God and his law (23:7–8)?*

- *What miraculous sign of the Lord's leadership and power did they witness together (vv. 3, 9–10)?*

- *What would determine their continued dominance in the land (v. 11)?*

When old Joshua called these leaders together at Shechem in the hill country of Ephraim near his home, they were all at least forty years younger than him. Still, they had many years of shared experience to reflect on. He could talk to them about what he had done, what God had done, and what they had done together. After all, God did not give them the land outright. They took possession of it as they cooperated with him. As long as they acknowledged the prominence of God in it, it was no contradiction to say that they all had a hand in the victory.

Knowing this, Joshua felt compelled to warn Israel just as Moses had warned them a generation ago. Keeping the land would be as challenging as getting the land.

Danger Ahead

• *What would happen if Israel turned aside to other alliances and their gods (vv. 12–13)?*

• *What word pictures did Joshua use to describe the way these nations would treat them? What predicament does each of these images suggest?*

• *What did Joshua mean when he said, "the way of all humanity" (v. 14)? Looking back over his lifetime, how does he summarize the Lord's fidelity to his promises?*

- *There was a hard edge to some of the promises that the Lord made to Israel. What promises did Israel not want the Lord to keep (vv. 15–16)?*

- *Does God's faithfulness demand that he keep all of his promises, even the harsh ones? Explain your answer.*

There was danger ahead—the danger of turning away from the Lord after he had brought them so far. The remaining inhabitants were weak and scattered. They were only a tiny remnant of the great peoples who were there when Israel arrived, but their continued residence in Canaan still presented danger.

If the Israelites befriended the Canaanites, if they adopted their ways, if they participated in their ceremonies or tolerated their religion, they would be coaxed away from God. And then they would be swept away by God. Making the choice to compromise in Canaan would uproot Israel from Canaan where God had planted them. The people remaining in Canaan would become snares, traps, whips, and thorns to Israel. And Israel would become hunted, captured, punished, wounded.

God's promises were true, all of them. He would keep his promises, all of them. The same God who tore this land away from the Canaanites for their idolatry would not spare Israel if they chose the same path.

- *In this final assembly, Joshua gathered everyone, but who would they hear from first (24:1–2)?*

- *As the Lord reviews Israel's history, what is the first idol worshiping mentioned (v. 2)? What ancestors did Joshua mention in the retelling (vv. 3–5)? Why was this history lesson key to what the Lord wanted to say?*

- *There are eight miracles listed in this history (vv. 6–12). Write down the ones that you find.*

- *How much credit could Israel take for their victories in the land (v. 12), the cities they were living in (v. 13), or the crops they were eating?*

By reminding Israel of their past, the Lord showed them how idolatry has never been far away. But he also showed them that he delivered them from the worship of other gods and bondage to the servants of other gods. By reminding them of their recent past, he taught them that loyalty to his covenant, made through Moses and renewed by Joshua, would provide them with continued success. It wasn't their abilities but God's power that gave them their ready-made inheritance. If they wanted to keep experiencing his provision, protection, and direction, they would have to remain with him.

Joshua's Challenge

- *Joshua charged Israel to follow his example in being faithful to the one true God. Whose idolatry does Joshua mention (vv. 14–15)?*

- *What choice did Joshua offer the people (vv. 14–15)?*
  Was it a real or rhetorical choice the people had to make?
  What choice did Joshua make for his whole household?

- *What commitment did the people make in response*
  to Joshua's challenge (v. 16)? What was the reasoning
  behind their choosing (vv. 17–18)?

- *What was Joshua's response to the declaration that the*
  people made (vv. 19–24)?

- *How did Joshua describe God's character? What do these attributes have to do with this choice Israel made? How would a God like that respond to idolatry?*

- *What was the final commitment of the people (v. 22)? As a result of that choice, what was their first obvious obligation (v. 23)?*

- *What two physical artifacts were created that day as constant reminders of Israel's choice (vv. 26–27)?*

Inertia and gravity are powerful forces of nature. One keeps things on their current trajectory or keeps them from moving at all. The other pulls things down. Spiritual inertia and gravity are genuine dangers, and Joshua's challenge to the people was meant to address those dangers.

Joshua and the Israelites engaged in a spiritual tug-of-war. He challenged them to choose the Lord. So they did. Or at least, they used words of commitment and devotion to the Lord. Joshua scoffed, saying that they could never keep such a promise. Almost offended, they assured him that they could. Again, he told them that he knew them too well to believe them. But the whole group fervently insisted that loyalty to the Lord was the choice they were determined to make.

Maybe today's evangelists could learn from Joshua's approach.

To seal the deal, Joshua made a written account of their covenant. He recorded it in the Book for posterity's sake. Then he took a large stone, a monument that would outlive them all, and erected it as a reminder of their commitment that day. The stone would stand there under the oak through each generation, a silent witness to what happened that day and how well Israel kept their public vows.

There Is a Choice

Joshua ended his era of leadership in Israel with this call to decision. They were now living in a land where Baal had been the chief god. The new people of the one true God came into this dangerous pagan setting. For the generation going forward without Joshua, there was a choice they had to make. Would they follow the Lord or the Baals? Would they love and serve the Lord wholeheartedly or only half-heartedly? Would they be faithful to their faithful God, or would they become spiritual adulterers?

There is always a choice to make because spiritual inertia and gravity are in every generation. Jesus' followers are surrounded by societies that are hostile toward their beliefs and lifestyle. Standing firm in such a setting takes a choice. Will we serve the Lord or compromise? Will we stay true to him in a dangerous cultural setting?

# DIGGING DEEPER

Human choice is a gift. A choice provides the opportunity for willing righteous action. A choice is the chance to get things right.

For Joshua, human beings who had the power to choose clearly had a decision to make. This was not merely a rhetorical device. Israel really could choose whether to serve the Lord.

There are many such choices presented in Scripture, moments of decision with real-world results. Read these representative passages. Which individual had a choice to make? What decision did they make? What were the obvious results of the decision?

Passage	Chooser	Choice	Outcome
Genesis 3:1–8			
Jonah 1:1–5			
Daniel 3:13–18			
Matthew 4:8–11			
Mark 1:16–20			
Mark 10:17–22			
Luke 22:54–62			
Acts 9:10–19			

Choosing Not to Choose Is a Choice

The Israelites responded to Joshua with fervent commitment. They didn't back down when he challenged the sincerity of their decision.

Five hundred years later, Elijah couldn't get their descendants to give even the simplest of answers. They wouldn't decide to be cold or hot toward God. They wanted to stay somewhere in the middle, lukewarm, tepid, room temperature.

Room temperature faith spoils like room temperature food. God spits it out (Revelation 3:15–16). He hates it. He wants us hot or cold. Make your choice.

Choosing not to choose means compromise. A lack of conviction or commitment makes us vulnerable to others with stronger convictions. That means the spiritual atmosphere around us will influence us. We will lose ground if we don't choose.

Choose and Choose Again

The Israelites made many choices in Joshua's era. They chose to follow a new leader. They chose to line up at the edge of a flooded river and walk through on dry ground. They chose to be circumcised as adults to renew their covenant. They chose to follow the strange strategy at Jericho. They chose to fight against vast armies. They chose to confront potential idolatry. They chose to renew their commitment when Joshua challenged them. They chose and chose and chose again.

We never stop choosing. We will always have the choice to draw near to God or wander off. We will always be choosing our loves, our priorities, our beliefs. We will always face temptation and the choice to obey or disobey. We will always choose.

The commitment to follow Jesus must happen daily: "If you truly desire to be my disciple, you must disown your life completely, embrace my 'cross' as your own, and surrender to my ways. For if you choose self-sacrifice, giving up your lives for my glory, you will discover true life. But if you choose to keep your lives for yourselves, you will lose what you try to keep" (Luke 9:23–24). Every day, we choose and choose again.

We are not left alone to make choices any more than Joshua and Israel were. God promised never to leave or forsake them (Joshua 1:5). In fact, the situation is even better for Christians who have the permanent presence of the Holy Spirit to guide us into everything that is true (John 16:13). We have his divine aid in every choice we make. With the Holy Spirit's power, we can always choose to follow Christ.

A great number of passages call us to depend on God's help as we walk forward with him. Match the first phrase with the second from the following sampling of Bible verses that teach this principle.

_____ He...leads me along in his footsteps of righteousness (Psalm 23:3)

A. to guide you, saying, "This is the right path; follow it."

_____ Escort me into your truth (Psalm 25:5)

B. we must also allow the Spirit to direct every aspect of our lives.

_____ Keep showing the humble your path (Psalm 25:9)

C. and keep you from bringing harm to yourself.

_____ He will lead us onward until the end (Psalm 48:14)

D. he will teach you all things in my name.

_____ Their wisdom will guide you wherever you go (Proverbs 6:22)

E. take me by the hand and teach me.

_____ You will hear his voice behind you (Isaiah 30:19–21)

F. and who leads you step by step in the way you should go.

_____ I am Yahweh, your mighty God! I grip your right hand and won't let you go! (Isaiah 41:13–14)

G. for it will lead you into truth, not a counterfeit.

_____ I will walk the blind by an unknown way (Isaiah 42:16)

H. I whisper to you: "Don't be afraid; I am here to help you!"

_____ I am Yahweh, your God. I am the One who teaches you how to succeed (Isaiah 48:17)

I. through all time, beyond death, and into eternity!

_____ When the Father sends the Spirit of Holiness (John 14:26)

J. so that I can bring honor to his name.

_____ If the Spirit is the source of our life (Galatians 5:25)

K. and guide them on paths they've never traveled.

_____ His anointing teaches you all that you need to know (1 John 2:27)

L. and lead them into the best decision.

Epilogue

• *How old was Joshua when he died (Joshua 24:29–30)? Compare this fact with Joseph's lifespan in Genesis 50:22–26. Where did Joseph lead the children of Israel to live? Where did Joshua lead the children of Israel to live?*

• *Did the people who publicly committed to follow the Lord do it (Joshua 24:31)? For how long were the Israelites faithful to God?*

• *Whose graveside service is finally held generations after his death (v. 32)? Who else died at the end of the book of Joshua (v. 33)? What was his role?*

Joshua's Israel made a strong choice that would carry them for a generation. They did not shrink back from his spiritual challenge. They committed themselves and their children to follow the ways of the Lord wholeheartedly and against the spiritual inertia and gravity of their own nature. However, as Elijah's showdown demonstrated, their national obedience wasn't permanent. It never is. They would need to choose and choose and choose again.

Sometime after Joshua's final challenge, another scribe collected all the writings by Joshua and about Joshua and placed them in this book. Then he carefully made a note about the funerals when Joshua, Joseph, and Eleazar, all men who believed God's promise, were laid to rest in the divinely given promised land.

For centuries now, Joshua's account of the conquest of Canaan has been challenging believers. Be strong and courageous to face every battle, trusting in Jesus Christ and growing in God's Word. Be faithful to the Lord because he is always faithful to us. Cooperate with him, and you will live up to the spiritual potential. Make the choice, every day, to take up your cross and follow him.

 EXPERIENCE GOD'S HEART

- *Do you find that following Jesus is getting easier or harder? What cultural or relational factors are making it so? Are you surrounded by people who encourage you in your faith or people who threaten it? What do you think Joshua would urge you to do in such situations?*

- *Where are you in your spiritual journey at the end of your study of Joshua? Do you need the challenge he gave to the Israelites? Are you in need of rededication to following the Lord? If so, do that now.*

♥ SHARE GOD'S HEART

- *Tell someone else about a time when you made a public profession of commitment to the Lord. What were the circumstances that led to that moment? Was it your first commitment to Jesus or a rededication?*

- *Pray for an opportunity to challenge a friend to follow and serve the Lord. It may be someone who is thinking about following Jesus. It may be someone who has wandered away for a while. It might be someone who is wavering. Play the role of Joshua; urge them to make a decision.*

Talking It Out

1. Joshua didn't pull the Israelites aside one at a time to issue this challenge. He called on the whole group to choose. As a result, Israel responded to Joshua's challenge as a whole nation. Together they would serve the Lord and obey him. Discuss the value of following Jesus as a community rather than just as individuals. Are there any pitfalls to it? How can walking with God as a group be helpful to each individual?

2. Share with each other two or three big ideas from this study of Joshua that will stick with you and help you walk forward with Jesus.

Endnotes

1. Brian Simmons et al., "A Note to Readers," *The Passion Translation: The New Testament with Psalms, Proverbs, and Song of Songs* (Savage, MN: BroadStreet Publishing Group, 2020), ix.

2. Charles Dickens, *A Christmas Carol* (London: Chapman & Hall, 1843), 7.

3. Francis A. Schaeffer, *Joshua and the Flow of Biblical History* (Downers Grove, IL: InterVarsity Press, 1975), 26–27.

4. Every four years the US presidential inauguration tableau represents a cross-section of American political culture. Curbed.com has an excellent collection of inauguration photos, paintings, and engravings from throughout US history. See Michelle Goldchain, "Past U.S. Inauguarations, Revealed in 45 Historic Photos," Curbed, January 9, 2017, https://dc.curbed.com/2017/1/9/14217350/inauguration-photo-rare-historic.

5   For more on the structure of Genesis and the role that the
     various family histories play in it, see P. J. Wiseman, *Ancient
     Records and the Structure of Genesis* (Nashville, TN: Thomas
     Nelson, 1985), and Roland K. Harrison, *Introduction to the
     Old Testament* (Grand Rapids, MI: William B. Eerdmans,
     1969), 543–53.

6   The biblical text seems to go out of its way to assure the
     reader that the purpose of the spies' visit was for shelter,
     not sex. The Hebrew phrases that usually imply fornication
     are missing from this telling. In contrast, the account of
     Samson in Gaza makes it obvious that he was there for
     prostitution (Judges 16:1).

7   DC Talk and The Voice of the Martyrs, *Jesus Freaks: Stories
     of Those Who Stood for Jesus* (Bloomington, MN: Bethany
     House, 1999), 52–55.

8   Some commentators even suggest that the negotiations
     (Joshua 2:17–20) took place while they dangled from the
     rope. See Trent C. Butler, *Word Biblical Commentary: Joshua*
     (Waco, TX: Word Books, 1983), 34.

9   These chapters about crossing over the Jordan are a complex harmonization of more than one report. It is as though two film crews were recording the events. The first crew submitted its footage for editing, and then the second did the same. Rather than cutting and splicing the footage, they are presented in a series. The result is a telling and retelling superimposed on each other. That is why, in the text, the priests block the water twice (Joshua 3:15–17; 4:10), people cross over twice (3:17; 4:10), the men carry stones and set them up twice (4:8–9, 19–20), the monuments are explained twice (vv. 5–7, 21–24), and the priests come out of the river twice (vv. 11, 15–18). Though there are syntactical clues indicating two accounts, the breaks between them are not always obvious, leading some commenters to believe that there were two stone pillars erected in Joshua 4. It seems more likely, however, that the same monument building is described twice. This multiple-point-of-view narrative happens elsewhere in Scripture, usually giving us additional insight into the recorded biblical events. The creation accounts of Genesis 1 and 2 are an example of this. The historical books of Kings and Chronicles (along with portions of Isaiah) also have this feature. So, too, do the New Testament Gospels.

10   Steve Goldman, "A Look into Pulse Theory and Why the Walls of Jericho Fell," Reliabilityweb.com, accessed December 15, 2022, https://reliabilityweb.com/articles/entry/a_look_into_pulse_theory_and_why_the_walls_of_jericho_fell.

11   G. Frederick Owen, "Archaeological Supplement,"
     Thompson Chain Reference Bible, (Indianapolis, IN: B. B.
     Kirkbride Bible Co., 1990).

12   Kathleen Mary Kenyon and Thomas A. Holland, *Excavations
     at Jericho*, 2 vols. (Israel: British School of Archaeology in
     Jerusalem, 1960).

13   Ian Volner, "Why Do People Build Walls? The Real Story of
     Jericho Offers a Surprising Answer," *Time*, May 30, 2019,
     excerpted from Ian Volner, *The Great Great Wall: Along the
     Borders of History from China to Mexico* (New York: Abrams
     Press, 2019), https://time.com/5597069/jericho-history.

14   Bryant G. Wood, "The Walls of Jericho," Associates for
     Biblical Research, June 9, 2008, https://biblearchaeology.
     org/research/chronological-categories/conquest-of-
     canaan/3625-the-walls-of-jericho.

15   Henry B. Smith Jr., "Archaeology's Lost Conquest," Answers
     in Genesis, July 1, 2014, https://answersingenesis.org/
     archaeology/archaeologys-lost-conquest.

16 You can learn more about archaeology and the Bible, including Jericho, here: B. G. Wood, "Did the Israelites Conquer Jericho?," *Biblical Archaeology Review 16, no. 2,* March–April 1990, 44–58; Richard S. Hess et al., eds., *Critical Issues in Early Israelite History* (Winona Lake, IN: Eisenbrauns, 2008); David Eldon Graves, *Biblical Archaeology: An Introduction with Recent Discoveries That Support the Reliability of the Bible*, vol. 1, 2nd ed. (Toronto, Canada: Electronic Christian Media, 2018), esp. chap. 4.

17 Richard Hess, *Joshua: An Introduction and Commentary* (Downers Grove, IL: InterVarsity Press, 1996), 176.

18 Brian Simmons, *The Books of Joshua, Judges, and Ruth*, The Passion Translation (Minneapolis, MN: Broadstreet Publishing, 2021), Joshua 7:25, note 'c.'

19 For more on this subject, see Paul Copan, *Is God a Moral Monster? Making Sense of the Old Testament God* (Grand Rapids, MI: Baker Book House, 2011); C. S. Cowles et al., *Show Them No Mercy: 4 Views on God and Canaanite Genocide* (Grand Rapids, MI: Zondervan, 2003); Susan Niditch, *War in the Hebrew Bible: A Study in the Ethics of Violence* (New York: Oxford University Press, 1995).

20 Etiology, pronounced EE-tee-ALL-uh-gee, is the study of causation. Usually, it refers to an explanation derived by observing the facts in the present. In history, it refers to the explanation of artifacts when the origins are uncertain. For example, when archaeologists originally researched ancient Irish round towers, they concluded that they were shelters from raids based on the observation that their doors were often high off the ground and accessible only by ladders. Later scholars questioned this etiology, noting that the construction would have made them death traps when invaders set fires around the base. Consequently, Irish round towers are almost universally acknowledged to have been bell towers for calling the faithful to prayer.

21 Of course, we know that not one tribe fully grew into its potential. The book of Joshua hints at this sad fact (15:63; 16:10; 17:12–13; 19:47), but the book of Judges explicitly detailed it at 1:19–2:5. The Lord gave them the land, conquered it with them, and divinely parceled it out to them. But he insisted on a partnership with them to subdue the whole land. He was faithful; they were not.

22 Cities of refuge were prescribed by the law. Moses explained the rationale for them and the process for accessing them in Numbers 35:6–29 and Deuteronomy 19:1–13. The description in Joshua is abbreviated because the concern here is limited to designating locations for this refuge.